CORBRIDGE – THE LAST TWO THOUSAND YEARS

To the memory of my parents, Alice Penelope and Robert Joicey Dickinson

CORBRIDGE

THE LAST
TWO THOUSAND YEARS

Gillian Dickinson

THE SPREDDEN PRESS

Contents:

First published November 2000
by The Spredden Press,
55 Noel Road, London N1 8HE
and distributed by
Smith Settle, Ilkley Road, Otley,
W. Yorkshire, LS21 3JP

ISBN 1 871739 96 9 (paperback)
ISBN 1 871739 91 8 (hardback)

British Library Cataloguing in
Publication Data:
A catalogue record is available
from the British Library

Designed by Gill Humphrys
Printed by Smith Settle

On the last night of 1900, eighty couples danced the night away in Corbridge's new Town Hall to celebrate the start of the 20th century. Otherwise nothing much happened in the village, apart from the usual first-footing. The villagers would have thought our welcome to the 21st century and the third millennium premature and perhaps its celebrations extravagant. So the end of the year 2000 seems quite a good moment to look back at the last century, much of whose history is part of the lives of older Corbridgeans; and, more briefly, to the start of Corbridge's recorded history, roughly two millennia ago.

History is a patchwork of our memories, our records and the things we have created or discarded. The Corbridge patchwork has many holes in it, long periods in the middle of our history where we know little apart from battles and devastation: most of our medieval records seem to have vanished in the Scottish wars. The Roman period has been studied in great detail and much

has been discovered in recent years, both by English Heritage and by Raymond Selkirk and his Northern Archaeology Group. There is the evidence of the buildings themselves, dating in Corbridge – the parish church of St Andrews – from the 7th century. There are records of Vestry Council meetings, church visitations and faculties though the parish deposits for Corbridge are very sparse. As we come nearer to the present there are family records; and two notable 19th-century historians (W.S.Gibson and Robert Forster) who knew people, themselves with long memories, who lived in the 18th century. There are early local guides, trade directories and, since 1895, the minutes of the Parish Council, set up by the Local Government Act of 1894. The County History, published in 1914, with a full volume devoted to Corbridge, incorporates a lot of original research on the earlier period, as the editors had access to all the relevant family papers as well as the Derwentwater deeds in

the Greenwich Hospital archives. There are also the beautiful maps of the Derwentwater holdings in Corbridge, made by the Greenwich Hospital surveyors in the 1730s and annotated later in the century.

But in recent history there are gaps though some individuals have done research on individual buildings and many people have useful records. Memories of daily life in the past century have to be disinterred from a variety of sources. For the late 19th and 20th centuries the files of the *Hexham Courant*, which started publication in 1865, are hugely useful, as are the private photographs of old Corbridge families, and the popular commercial photographs of early photographers.

In this short account I have used what sources I could find to illustrate some aspects of life in the village of Corbridge. It is intended for the general reader but I hope some of the research I have done, referenced in notes at the end, may interest other historians

It was curiosity that encouraged

me to discover more about Corbridge history than is readily available. I was born just outside Corbridge, went to church with the family in St Andrews and to a little pre-prep school up the Aydon Road run by Miss Cochrane. My own early memories of the war include the evacuees who stayed with us; collecting my gas mask from the ARP (Air Raid Precautions) centre in the Pele Tower; and the Italian prisoners-of-war. One of them gardened for us and, like most Italians, he loved children, and he made toys for us out of odd pieces of wood. Soon after the war, when bananas first came into the shops, our grandmother gave my brother and me a penny each to buy a banana or an orange. Neither of us could remember what a banana looked like and I played safe and chose an orange.

After a long time away, I returned last year to live in Watling Street, in a house which had belonged to one of Corbridge's oldest families– the Surtees Forsters – since at least the late

19th century. Mrs Fairless (née Surtees Forster) lived with her grandmother for five years in the 1930s while she went to Hexham Grammar School and she showed me the layout of the house and shop. Her uncle was the youngest labourer on the Corstopitum excavation of 1907, the one that discovered the Corbridge Lion. Mrs Fairless's father, Mr Hornsby, had been chauffeur to F.M.Laing of Farnley Grange, a dealer in wines and spirits, and it was he who managed to obtain the land to build Corbridge's Town Hall.

But who was the architect of that attractive building? The detective story began...

Many people have helped me with encouragement, information or illustrations but I would like particularly to thank John Bishop, Bob Douglas, Mrs D. Fairless, George Hall, John Malden (the Rex Malden Archive), Frank Soulsby and Sue Moon for the loan of their precious photographs. John Malden also allowed me to use the watercolours by Lucy

Gipps that appear on the covers of this book. Corine Emley gave me details of the life of her grandfather, Frank Emley, and provided me with books and photographs. Several historians have helped me, in particular Dr John Blair, Claude Blair, Georgina Plowright, Peter Ryder and Raymond Selkirk. I would also like to thank Claud Bicknell, M.C. Bishop, John Clark, Dr Bill Cunningham, John Gall, Andrew Gillam, Mrs Graddol, David Nicol, David Walton, Mrs D. Young and Mrs Joyce Young for information or the loan of books. And a special thank you to my old neighbour, Collin Forster, for his encouragement and life-long memories of Corbridge.

I owe a great debt to the staff of Corbridge and Hexham Libraries and the *Hexham Courant* for their assistance; the Librarian of the Society of Antiquaries, London; Beverley Cole of the National Railway Museum; the staff of the British Newspaper Library, the Map Room at the British Library,

the Public Record Office, the Society of Antiquaries, Newcastle upon Tyne, the Northumberland Record Office, the Library of the Royal Institute of British Architects (RIBA), and the Local Studies Section of Newcastle City Library. There are bound to be mistakes, either of understanding or fact, and I should be grateful for any corrections.

The following organizations and individuals have given me permission to use photographs in copyright or in their possession (numbers refer to captions). The British Library 2; Museum of Antiquities of the University and Society of Antiquaries of Newcastle upon Tyne, 5; Trustees of Corbridge Excavation Fund, 7 8; Society of Antiquaries of Newcastle upon Tyne, 9; National Railways Museum, 64, 166, 168; Beamish The North of England Open Air Museum, 66, 72, 176-9; Northumberland Record Office, 17 (photo reproduced in Robin Gard, Northumberland Yesteryear); Newcastle Libraries

and Information Service, 15, 21, 85, 140; Barclays Group Archives, 120, 142; Lloyds Bank plc Group Archives, 121; Marshall Hall and Anderson and Garland, 79; *Hexham Courant*, 165; Rex Malden Archive, 18, 19 24-6, 33, 39, 40, 78, 84, 95, 96, 100-1, 108-10, 122, 132, 150, 152-3, 155-6, 159, 164, 169; Bob Douglas, 41-2, 46-7, 51, 55, 57, 59, 60-1, 63, 75, 87-90, 94, 111-2, 114, 123-7, 141, 167, 182; Corbridge Village Trust, 23, 37, 43, 45, 56, 58-9, 62, 77, 91, 103, 113, 136, 157, 160, 173; Women's Institute, Corbridge Branch, 52; Mrs D.Fairless, 10, 11, 129, 133; Frank Soulsby 65, 67a-c, 69-71, 80-2, 130-1, 135, 137-8, 162-3, 171, 180-2; George Hall, 44, 48-50, 83, 115-7, 118-9, 134, 139; John Bishop, 53, 54, 104, 105; Mrs J. Moon. 93, 106, 107; Raymond Selkirk, 3, 4, 6; Julie Chesser, 34, Corine Emley, 144-9. The following are from *History of Northumberland,* vol. 10: 12, 16, 20, 22, 27, 99.

1. Aerial view of village from east, c.1960

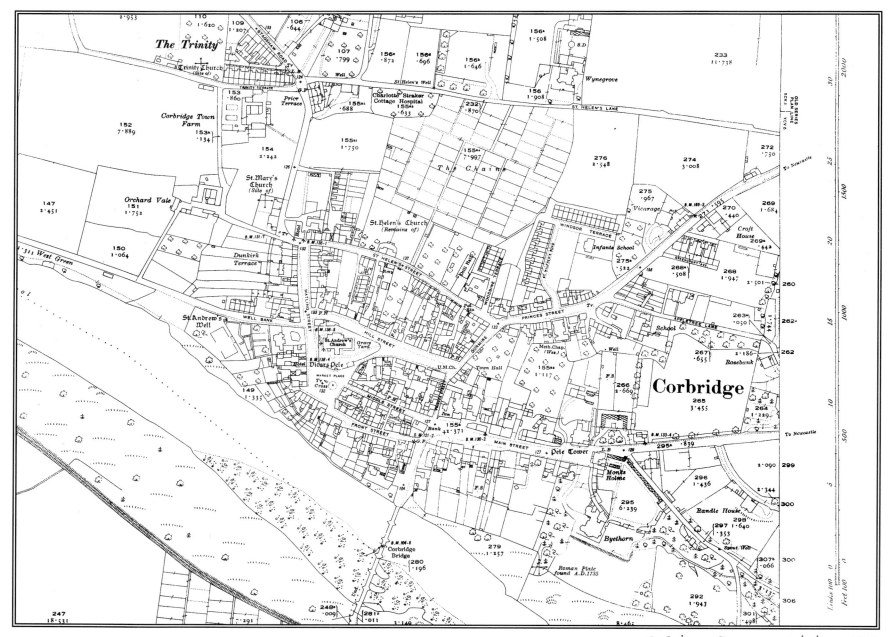

2. Ordnance Survey map, 3rd edition, 1922

Here is a natural amphitheatre, stepped into terraces by the constantly changing course of the Tyne, requiring to be peopled[1]

The Story

The Romans and after

We now know that there has been mixed farming in the Tyne valley for many thousands of years. Evidence has been found at Corbridge of pre-Roman ploughing; the site of a native farmstead at Apperley Dene beside Dere Street, near Stocksfield, has been identified, and over the years many objects have been found. An encampment at Shildon, north of Corbridge, was excavated in 1964. And beneath the main Corbridge site have been found the circular ditch and postholes of an earlier settlement.

The Roman period is the most studied in our history and every year there are new theories about the roads and the bridges which were the principle reason for the importance of Corbridge to the Romans, an importance which has lasted throughout our history. The roads were probably laid out by Julius Agricola, the Roman governor, or his immediate successors, and have recently been studied extensively by Raymond Selkirk who claims to have discovered a very much larger network of Roman roads than had hitherto been suspected.

Dere Street, the principal route, ran north from the military HQ at York to Corbridge where a fort was built to guard the crossing

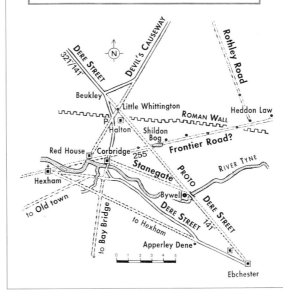

LOST ROMAN ROADS
OF THE
TYNE VALLEY

over the Tyne, and thence to Scotland. Selkirk's investigated 'lost' road, Proto Dere Street, continues in a straight line south from Beukley to Ebchester and crosses the road known as the Devil's Causeway at Little Whittington. Proto Devil's Causeway runs to the first Roman camp at Beaufront Red House,[2] established by Agricola in 79AD and excavated in 1974. A river crossing has been found here, a mile upstream from the known Roman bridge. Just downstream from this bridge, whose few remains can be seen on the south side of the river upstream from the present bridge, a Roman jetty (? see fn .13) and weir have been discovered.

The Stanegate ran east and west, and its route from Carlisle to

3. Remaining stones from south abutment of Roman bridge

4. Map by Raymond Selkirk of suspected lost Roman roads

Corbridge has long been known. Raymond Selkirk has now traced the road east beyond Corbridge to Bywell,[3] where he believes there was a Roman bridge, and Ovingham.

A site to the east of the Red House, known as Bishop Rigg, was also excavated in 1974 and found to contain a some timber enclosures, possibly pre-Roman, a temporary Roman camp and Roman gravel quarries.[4]

The Roman Site

The present Roman site at Corbridge, now in the care of English Heritage, is all that remains of what was once a major Roman town dating from the early third century. It had a central water supply, a large courtyard building, granaries, houses and workshops as well as compounds for a small military garrison, and at least two cemeteries[5]. However, excavations between 1934 and 1980, published in a series of reports, have revealed that this town – its name is now known to be Coria, not Corstopitum – was preceded by a succession of Roman forts, one on top of another.

The first fort on the Corbridge site was built as part of Agricola's consolidation of his victory over the Scottish tribes at Mons Graupius (? on the Moray Firth) in 84AD and contained a

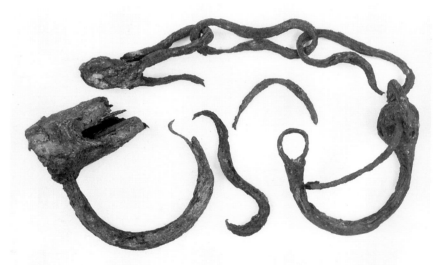

5. Aemilia ring, late 2nd to 4th century AD. Found at west end of Corstopitum in January 1840. The letters round the middle read 'Aemilia zeses' (Long life to Aemilia). Probably a wedding or betrothal ring.

6. Slave manacles discovered near Roman bridge suggesting Romans used slave labour for construction or maintenance of bridge. The barrel lock is made of bronze

7. The Corbridge Lanx, a silver salver (c. 4th century) was found in February 1734 by the daughter of a Corbridge blacksmith, Thomas Cutter, on the north side of the river, about 150 yards below the bridge.

Cutter sold it to Isaac Cookson, goldsmith of Newcastle, and it was subsequently claimed by the Lord of the Manor, the Duke of Somerset. Now British Museum. Photograph taken c.1950.

headquarters building, a hospital, a large granary block and a barrack block. This fort was modified and eventually destroyed c.105 by fire. In the charred remains in the west range of the hospital was found a chest containing several pieces of armour which has provided important evidence of how the legionaries were protected and armed. The last fort was built c.139 at the time of the construction of the turf wall, known as the Antonine Wall, between the Forth and the Clyde. It was dismantled in 163 when the forts on Hadrian's Wall were once again filled with troops[6].

After the Romans finally abandoned the town, in the 4th century, the stone was used, for centuries, as a valuable quarry. Builders from the 7th century knew of it and St Andrews, Corbridge's parish church, the Vicar's Pele and many houses in the village benefited from its finely dressed stones. Treasure hunters also plundered the site for gold, most notably King John who found nothing.

In the 18th century there were still walls standing above ground but in about 1800 the then Duke of Northumberland cleared the south-west part of the site for cultivation and some of the stones were used to rebuild Corbridge Mill[7]. The historian Robert Forster, writing in the 1880s, recalls that 'a few years ago' stones were used to build the bridge across the Corburn, (i.e. the southern bridge near the Roman site). Others were taken from the ruins of St Helen's chapel, part of the old manorial hall in Hall-Garth whose foundations are behind our Parish Hall[8].

8. Robert Forster, outside site museum with trug full of finds

9. Young worker delivers trugs, used for collecting finds, during 1910 excavations.

An Edwardian Excavation[9]

The first archaeological excavation took place in 1906 as the result of a decision by the History of Northumberland committee, chaired by Professor Haverfield, to publish a volume on Corbridge and thanks to the support and enthusiasm of the landowner, Captain Cuthbert of Beaufront. The 1906 season was supervised by Leonard Woolley, later to become famous for his work in the Near East, but in 1907 his assistants, Robert Forster and W.H.Knowles, took charge. Forster, who supervised the work, had been born in Corbridge, the son of a mining engineer, and was a respected archaeologist who had also been a barrister, novelist and poet.

He seems to have been popular with the labourers he recruited, all local men with no training in archaeology. It was hard work, with the pick and shovel, and many tons of topsoil had to be

ROMAN LION, CORBRIDGE.

10. The Corbridge Lion was found in a cistern, or water tank, behind a large building on the south-west of the Roman site. All the coping stones probably came from a funerary monument although the Lion was re-used as a fountain.

removed to uncover the remains and then replaced afterwards. To begin with there were six to nine men but the group photo shown here, taken just after the discovery of the Corbridge Lion, shows twenty-five men and one boy. The boy is Surtees Forster, who had just left school, aged fourteen. He became a Sergeant in the Northumberland Fusiliers and was killed, nine years later, in the First World War.

Many fragments of stone sculptures were discovered, often re-used by the Romans as building material. In 1907 a small packet of 48 gold coins was found wrapped, with a gold ring, in a piece of sheet lead. These, with the Corbridge Lanx, discovered on the north bank of the Tyne in 1734, are now in the British Museum.

The man in charge of the photographic record of this excavation was J.P.Gibson, the Hexham pharmacist who had, by now, a flourishing photographic business and gave lectures on this still relatively new discovery. He made postcards from his photographs and these were sold to visitors to the site.

11. Labourers on the 1907 excavations at Corstopitum, taken on the day that the Corbridge Lion was discovered.

The young boy in the front is Surtees Forster, aged 14, and the man on his right in the second row is George William Hall, grandfather of the butcher, George Hall

Anglo-Saxon Corbridge

Roman authority broke down in the late 4th century though some kind of activity at the Roman site may have continued into the 5th century. The earliest settlement on the present site of Corbridge seems to date from the 7th century and it was a Christian one.

According to his biographer, St Wilfrid built the priory church at Hexham from 675-80AD and it is very likely that the church of St Andrew in Corbridge and, possibly those dedicated to St Andrew at Bywell and Heddon, had direct connections with St Wilfrid, for St Andrew was his favourite saint. This might imply that the churches were started in his lifetime. Certainly, by 700 'the Tyne Valley in particular was..a focus of Bernician Christian activity'[10].

However, the first reference to the Anglian settlement and St Andrew's church is in 786. In that year Et Corabrige, one of the many names by which Corbridge became known, is mentioned in the Northumbrian Annals as a 'monastery' where the bishop Aldulf was consecrated.

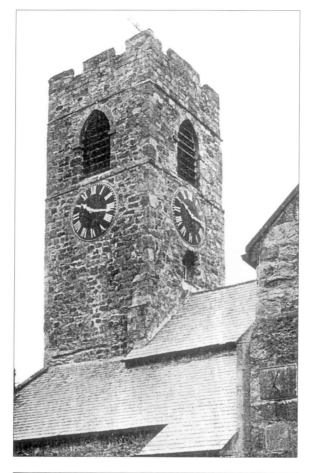

12. Saxon tower, showing original gable, from History of Northumberland

13. Roman arch in St Andrew's Church

14. Saxon eagle on north side of St Andrew's tower.

15. (opposite) Norman door of church, c.1300, before the addition of porch (1919).

The lay-out of the village, half a mile east of the Roman settlement, suggests that Corbridge began as a minster (Anglo-Saxon for monastery) consisting simply of groups of monks, nuns or priests living in wooden huts within an enclosure[11]. Later this ditch (see map p.19) would become the boundary of the medieval settlement. The church, 'the most important surviving Saxon Monument in Northumberland, except for Hexham crypt'[12], was built largely of stones from the Roman site, with a narrow aisleless nave, a chancel and a western porch which developed into the lower part of the tower, probably in the late 7th century – the blocked western door is still visible. The tower arch, leading into the nave, was removed in its entirety from a Roman building.

The upper part of the tower is now dated to the early 11th century, a century when fine towers were also built at Warden, Bywell St Andrew and Ovingham: A Saxon eagle has been identified on the north face. There are Saxon stones in the side walls of the nave, above the arcades, and a number of Saxon stones and parts of grave slabs and a finial cross are still in the church or Pele tower, or in the private house constructed out of the Viney museum. The original west gable window (see opposite) is now in the eastern wall of the tower.

Watermill discovery

A structure on the north side of the Roman bridge has recently been identified as an Anglo-Saxon watermill with a wheel house floor of dressed blocks taken from the Roman bridge and a timber waterchute. If the identification, which is still controversial,[13] is confirmed it is an extremely important discovery for little is known of the secular aspects of settlement in the north-east before the 11th century.

A Crown Manor and its Church

Corbridge became one of the royal towns that was part of the Anglian kingdom of Northumbria as early as the 8th century. The Danish invasions of the 9th and 10th centuries probably destroyed most of the minster. Northumbria ceased to be a kingdom and pledged fealty as an earldom to the kings of Wessex. It became a Crown manor again after the earldom was extinguished in 1095.

A very small community of priests probably remained to serve the church which became part of the royal demesne. In 1122 Henry I granted four Northumbrian churches, including Corbridge, with lands and the major tithes, to Richard d'Orival for life, with reversion to the new Augustinian priory of St Mary at Carlisle. Later in this century the south door, with its dog-toothed ornament, would have been built – perhaps at the same time as the Trinity church built by the prior.

An undated pre-Reformation survey gives the acreage of the prior's Rectory as 138 acres of arable. These were held by the prior and convent until the priory was dissolved in the 16th century, and subsequently by the dean and chapter of Carlisle who still have the gift of St Andrew's – they appoint the vicar.

The tenants of the priory had their houses on the Stagshaw road, outside the defensive ditch and near the manor house whose name survives in Prior Mains. It had its own court and its own church, dedicated to the Trinity. Though the first mention of the church is in the 14th century, about a dozen stones of a Norman plinth were found, apparently from the nave of the chapel, when Trinity Terrace was being built in 1888.

The Vicarage

A vicarage was built about 1195, when the archdeacon of Carlisle (appointed by the Prior) was acting as parson. It was also outside the defensive ditch, but on the east side of the township and was valued, with its glebe land and tithes, in 1254 at 12 marks (£380). A terrier of 1662 described the 'vicarage dwelling-house only bounded on the south with the street called Prince Street, on the west with the yard belonging to the said house, on the east and on the north with the lands belonging to Cuthbert Redhead' and various other holdings including the churchyard belonging to Trinity church. This is also mentioned as a possession of the vicarage in later valuations of the glebe.

It would be interesting to know for how long Trinity's burial ground was used: a large number of bodies has been found here at various times in the 19th century and 20th centuries. Could Trinity churchyard ever have been used as an adjunct to St Andrew's graveyard after it became part of the holdings of the vicar and Trinity church was no longer used?

The Vicar's Pele

The Vicar's Pele was presumably built (largely of stones from the Roman site) to give the vicar greater protection than he had in his vicarage. It had a vaulted basement used for storage and two upper floors.

It is probably the best preserved tower house in Northumberland and unusual in that it always stood alone, and was not attached to a larger house like most so-called 'pele towers'. I always think it demonstrates something of the then vicar's cavalier attitude towards his flock: he would leave them outside when the Scots visited, used dozens of their gravestones as building material, and even had his personal privy simply emptying into the churchyard. One of the medieval gravestones re-used, as the inner lintel of the smaller of the two windows on the south of the first floor, has a cross identical to that of the 'Lady Alice' gravestone in the church.[14]

Corbridge's Townships

The manor seems to have been the central part of a great royal estate that embraced the whole of middle Tyneside. This manor once included nine townships - roughly equivalent to the territorial divisions of the earldom - whose parish church was St Andrews. These are Corbridge, Dilston, Thornborough, Aydon Castle, Aydon, Little Whittington, Halton, Clarewood with Halton Shields and Great Whittington, the three last forming the dependent chapelry of Halton and they are still part of the ecclesiastical parish. They became distinct farming communities but they pastured on a common moor and the lord's church and court were in Corbridge, the largest vill[15].

Corbridge Pele Tower. Drawing by W. J. Palmer from The Tyne and its Tributaries

A Taste of Prosperity

The 13th century was probably Corbridge's finest time. In 1201 King John visited Northumberland and granted charters to Corbridge, Hartlepool, Newcastle, Rothbury and Alnwick, allowing them the privilege of farming their own towns in return for a payment. It was a great period for church building in Tynedale: large parts of the churches of Haltwhistle, Warden, Bywell, Ovingham and Heddon on the Wall, as well as Hexham Priory, were built in this century. St Andrews was given a new chancel and transepts, and fine lancet windows at the east end, in three successive phases of enlargement which brought the building to its present dimensions.

In 1235 the burgesses began to build a new bridge, as the Roman one had long ceased to be useable, upstream from the present bridge. This promoted trade and by 1296 Corbridge was the second wealthiest town in Northumberland after Newcastle – and Newcastle was the fifth richest in England. And in 1295 Corbridge sent two burgesses to Parliament, though the summons was never repeated. Corbridge was never a parliamentary borough.

The Stagshaw Fair, which was to last until 1929[16], had started by 1204 when the manor of Corbridge was granted to Robert fitz Roger with the privilege of a weekly market, and an annual fair on the eve, day, and day after the Feast of St John the Baptist (24 June).

From a 19th-century description of the Stagshaw Fair

The Duke's officials proceeded from the Angel Inn to the Market Cross where the proclamation was read by the manor bailiff or his deputy declaring and defining the rights and prerogatives of the lord of the manor..

This fair, which was one of business as well as pleasure, was the largest held in England for one day, and for business people came to it from all parts of the country. Besides horse, sheep, cattle and swine, various articles of merchandise were offered...men's hats, boots and shoes...the former mostly from Hexham and a considerable quantity of the latter from Corbridge. Jewellery and hardware stalls were prominent; saddlery and farming goods such as hay rakes, forks etc were always plentiful, and always a large supply of cooperage goods,

such as tubs, barrels, churns etc. Webs of cloth, coarse and fine, were shown to advantage on the green carpet by the side of the pond...

16. Reading the rules at Stagshaw Fair, Ralph Hedley, 1882
17. Crowd at proclamation of Stagshaw Fair, c.1910

On the south side of the horse fair there was an auction of watches, being for the most part forfeited pledges...There was a supply of bee skeps.

From a long row of gingerbread and orange stalls could be heard some dame crying out lustily 'Boole up and buy a way', others were shouting at the top of their voice 'London spice twopence a package', while others displayed along the length of their arm twenty-four squares of gingerbread offered at a shilling the lot: oranges, cherries, Barcelona nuts etc. were plentiful...

In addition to what was consumed in the fair, immense quantities were carried home for it was the custom for almost everyone to do so, carrying it in their pockets or handkerchiefs (for there were no bags in those days) and this was called their 'fair'[17].

Highland drovers

It was naturally much frequented by Scots and Bailey and Culley recorded in 1797 that in the early part of the century, J.M.Bates, of Aydon White House, bought a Gaelic grammar in order to acquire enough of the language to converse with the Highland drovers of Stagshaw Bank who could hardly speak any English'[18].

Border Warfare

At the end of the 13th century peace came to an end and what one historian[19] has called the Three Hundred Years' War began between England and Scotland. In April 1296 a force of men from Galloway, led by seven Scottish earls, burnt Hexham priory, the grammar school with 200 boys within it, then moved on to destroy Corbridge and much of its church. The following year, in November, Wallace occupied Hexham, and marched along the north bank of the Tyne, burning Bywell and probably harming Corbridge as well. The bridge became impassable. Corbridge was again burnt in 1312. In 1346 David Bruce, taking advantage of Edward III's absence in France, marched on Hexham and, although Corbridge was saved, many small hamlets in the surrounding country were destroyed, never to recover. Devastation was followed by the Black Death which depopulated the manor of Styford. The Vicar's Pele was probably built in the early 14th century as a fortified vicarage. Popular tradition stated that the lower or arched story was used for the safe keeping of the Vicar's cow;[20] in fact, besides being a storehouse, it probably sheltered many cattle from Scottish raids.

Corbridge in the 14th century

The County History quotes two contemporary surveys[21] to describe the Corbridge of the late 14th century, after a kind of peace had returned. In the middle of the market place was the Market Cross and it was from the steps of this Cross that the Stagshaw Fair was proclaimed. To the north of the church stood the Tolbooth, or Court House. There was a

fountain to which water was brought in a lead pipe from a spring to the east of the village. The Market Place was surrounded by shops and booths, partly hiding the parish church. Backing on to the churchyard was the Vicar's Pele. To the north-west Marketgate led into Westgate (Watling Street). St Helen's Lane (now St Helen's Street) ran from the north end of Westgate, past the remains of the manor hall, the Hall-Garth and its private chapel, dedicated to St Helen, into Prent Street (now Princes Street).

Streets led east and west from

18. Sculpted heads on the south wall of the west end of the nave. St Andrews Church

19. Sculpted heads outside the Wheatsheaf Hotel

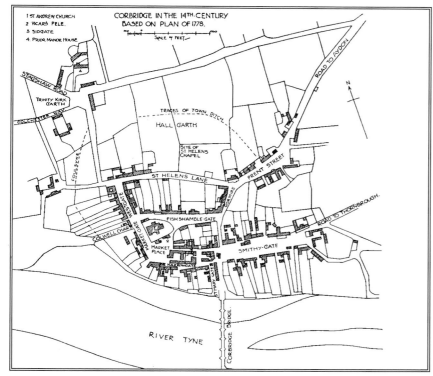

CORBRIDGE PELE DOOR 212

CORBRIDGE MARKET CROSS.

the junction of Westgate and Marketgate. The modern Wellbank was known as Colwell-chare, from the Colwell or Corwell by the roadside. It was down this lane that the Carelgate, the ancient high road from Newcastle to Carlisle, passed out of the town on the west. It ran past the Corbridge Mill, near the south-west corner of the Roman station: this was the lower of the two 'water corn mills' to which the villagers took their corn to be ground before baking it in the King's Oven in the Market

Place. Both mills belonged to the Duke but in 1869 the Corbridge Mill (the only one still standing) was sold to William Cuthbert who, under a lease of 1783, re-let it to the occupier, Robert Richley. His family had occupied the mill for 300 years[22].

Until 1895, when the first Parish Council changed the names, the west end of Hill Street was known as Scramblegate (earlier Fishshamblegate, and before that Fishmarketgate, Horsemarket Street and

Hidemarket) and the eastern part as Heron's Hill.

To the east of the Market place ran Sidgate (Middle Street) and Narrowgate (later Water Row and now Front Street). There was a toll bar on the north side of the bridge and a street called Marygate (from the chapel of St Mary on the bridge, now St Mary's Chare or the Bad Bank) ran north from it to Narrowgate and Sidgate.. The road past the Coigns, as far as the junction of Prent Street and

St Helen's Lane, was known as Gormire.

20. Map of Corbridge Township in the 14th century.

21. Pele tower door showing medieval grille. Photo, c. 1920

22. Old Market Cross, 13th century, on its Roman altar. Removed by John Walker of Eastfield and presented to the Society of Antiquaries of Newcastle upon Tyne in 1924. Drawing by Robert Bertram

Our Main Street was commonly known as Smithygate, the place where ironworking – a large industry in Corbridge – was carried on. One specimen of the art of English (?Corbridge) smiths at this time is the iron grille backing the oak door of the Vicar's Pele.[23] There was a tanning industry and evidence of early lime-burning was discovered in the village when, in 1890, the Old Blue Bell Inn was pulled down.

There were several large freeholders in Corbridge from an early period. One of these was the Baxter family who built the tower of Low Hall. The manor of Corbridge was granted by the king to Lord Percy of Alnwick in 1332 but the family lost it to the Carnaby family after the northern rebellion in 1536, known as the Pilgrimage of Grace. A grant of lands to St Margaret's chapel, Durham, was given on perpetual lease to Roger Heron of Hallington and eight generations of this family lived in Corbridge, giving their name to Heron's Hill.

Problems for Travellers

The bridge was in a constant state of disrepair and the countryside must have been dangerous to travellers. There is an account of

CORBRIDGE from the River Tyne

Lord Chief Justice North travelling the circuit during the reign of Charles II, in the late 17th century. His road ran through Bywell 'which was inhabited by expert handcraftsmen who worked in iron: village blacksmiths who became inured to be armed; and the tenants of each manor in the barony of Bywell being bound to guard the judges in their progress, the service devolved on these stout and hardy men'[24]. The Lord Chief Justice describes his attendants as wearing long beards, short cloaks and long basket-hilted broadswords, hanging from broad belts and mounted on horses so small that the riders' feet and swords touched the ground.

Goods were carried along the Carelgate in single-horse carts travelling in convoy for protection, like an Eastern caravan. But in 1663 the first Turnpike Act was passed and, by obliging road users to pay for their maintenance,

23. (opposite) The Carelgate, the old road to Carlisle on the north side of the river, c.1910

24. Mill field. The water would have been led down the line of the fence by a wooden waterchute

25. Corbridge Mill, c.1970, showing entrance for water (window above door). The medieval building was rebuilt in 1804 using stones from the Roman site and St Helen's Church

There are four sundials in the village:

26a. Low Hall, front of house, dated 1700;

26b. Bridge, on the right-hand wall when entering from the south, dated 1674, the date of the bridge;

26c. Church, south wall of the south transept, dated 1694;

26d. Angel Inn, over main door, dated 1726

these Acts gradually brought a great improvement to the major roads. However, in Northumberland this did not happen until after the 1745 Jacobite rebellion. The troops had found the old Carelgate almost impassable and, as a result, a new Military Road was constructed in 1751, later connected to Corbridge via Aydon.

In 1674 a new bridge was built at Corbridge, the only one on the Tyne to survive the great flood of 1770.

Turnips and Potatoes

What John Grey (the renowned Receiver and Agent of Greenwich Hospital's Northern Estates) called 'that blessed union' between Scotland and England was achieved in 1707; the Crowns had been united in 1603. The Borders still had to suffer the Stuart rebellions of 1715 and 1745 but there were fewer raids and the growing security of property allowed some improvements in agriculture. Much of the land was waste and undrained and few crops were grown. According to Gibson, writing in 1862, 'only a century ago no turnips were grown in Northumberland and the culture of potatoes was then first introduced by the vicar of the Border parish of Norham'[25]. In the 19th century Corbridge potatoes would become famous, commanding the highest prices in the Newcastle market.

Enclosure

It was the ending of the medieval system of agriculture by which individuals owned strips of land 'dispersed and intermixed' that allowed farming on a more economic scale. This general enclosure, as it was called, came much later in Northumberland than in more settled southern counties. In the earliest times, all the cultivated lands of Corbridge were north of the river; south of the Tyne was common and waste. Dilston was an early enclosure out of forest, as were the farms of the Linnels, Farnley and the Eales. But the township of Corbridge remained unenclosed until the late 18th century. As the Vicar, the Rev. John Walton senior, implored the Duke of Somerset (lord of the manor) in 1724, 'We of this township enjoy an healthful air and as rich and sweet a soil as any place in this county...yet scarce producing

27. Part of Plan of Corbridge and Dilston from History of Northumberland to illustrate the Common Field system in 1776.

food for its inhabitants... And when it pleases God to send good crops we lose much of them again by the damage done by cattle, the trespasses of travellers and of one another in tracing through other people's ridges in order to come at our own'[26].

His pleading, and that of others, was eventually successful: in 1776 an Act of Parliament authorised a general enclosure of the whole township with a few exceptions which included part of Stagshaw Bank. A map was made of the Award, as it came to be known, and this was constantly referred to whenever there were disputes over land rights[27]. In 1879 the people of Corbridge, using the Award, won a famous court case in Newcastle, establishing the public right of way through ancient common land known then as the Plantations (because of the wood planted by the Greenwich Hospital Comissioners) but previously as the Saughs. Evidence proved that the land had never belonged to the Earl of Derwentwater and therefore Greenwich Hospital had no right to it.[28] An important witness was Willie Jordan, the carter, then aged seventy-eight (photo page 68).

The Derwentwater Estates and Greenwich Hospital

The much-loved 3rd Earl was executed on Tower Hill on 24 February, 1715. Omens were seen in the sky and any object connected with the Earl became a revered relic. His huge estate was seized by the Crown and settled by George II, in 1735, on Greenwich Hospital which had been established in 1695 'for the relief and support of seamen'. Greenwich's Commissioners obtained, in 1738, an Act of Parliament, authorizing them to exchange, with the Duke of Northumberland, forty acres in the common fields of Corbridge for land in Alnwick and Warkworth.

However, the legal situation was extremely complicated: the estates were held by trustees until 1776, and large sums of money had to be paid to various members of the Earl's family, the Radcliffes. Dilston Hall was demolished by the Commissioners in 1765, the stone sold – some being used to build the Golden Lion pub, Corbridge House and Riverdale (previously the Radcliffe Hotel) – and the Earl's possessions dispersed. Many objects, notably a

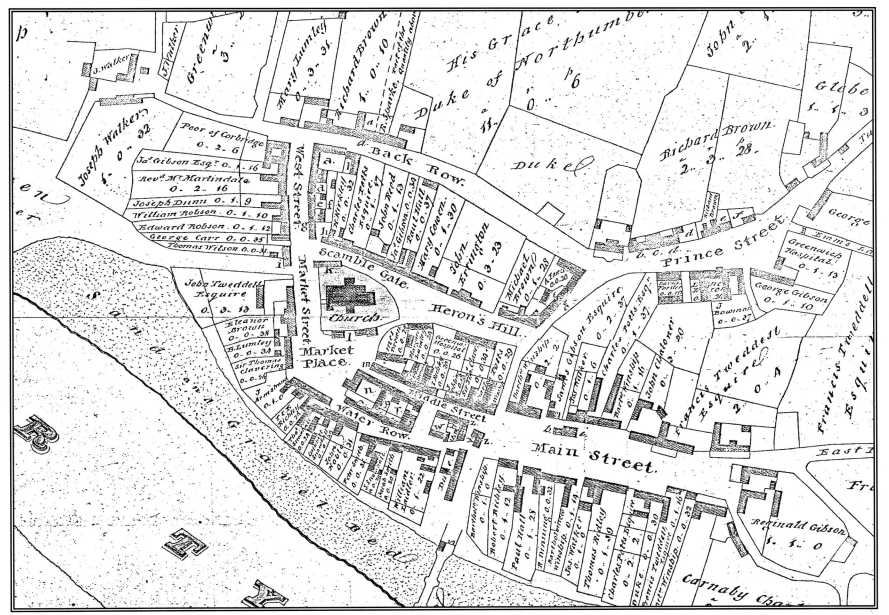

28. Tithe map c.1780,(owner untraced) showing holdings in village. Note vicarage, an L-shaped building north of Prince Street in Vicar's Glebe, demolished 1831

large oak table, found their way into Corbridge homes.

The Earl's Possessions

We recollect many years ago being shown two or more standing or case clocks which were brought from Dilston Hall, but they are not now in the neighbourhood... The late Mr Surtees of Corbridge had the spice box from the still room or kitchen, made of mahogany and used for keeping the different kinds of spices...

The late Mr George Tweddell had a beautiful copper coffee pot...

Miss Charlton of Corbridge has a painting on glass of the head and shoulders of the Earl; it belonged to her uncle the late Mr Joseph Dodd, brought from Dilston Hall in the original frame which is carved and had been silvered or gilded.[29]

John Grey of Dilston

Parts of the estate had already been sold off, including some beautiful property on the banks of Derwentwater, when John Grey (1785-1868) was appointed Receiver and Agent of the Northern Estates of the Greenwich Hospital in 1833. It was said at the time that his appointment was political, the reward for his strong support for his cousin Earl Grey during the passing of the Reform Bill of 1832 and for the other Whig causes of free trade, anti-slavery and Catholic Emancipation. But he had long experience and a deep knowledge of agriculture and occupied his post with great distinction until his retirement in 1863 when he had become known, throughout the country, as 'a leading name in English agriculture'. He found a great deal of corruption in the management of the estate and 'had to dismiss about 200 tradespeople of various kinds, and value the building requirements to be done, which were numberless, and this of course in the face of those who had lived on the plunder of the estates'. This cannot have been easy and his daughter and biographer, Josephine Butler, quotes an old friend saying that

He was denounced in the most scurrilous manner in all the Tory papers, as well as by many jobbers who saw their fate impending. So bad was it that Mr (Henry) Gipps, the vicar, not then a very sympathising friend, was thoroughly ashamed of the tactics of his party and much to his credit...(declared) his personal knowledge of the

upright, honest and efficient way in which Mr Grey administered the Hospital estates, without partiality or political bias...This put an end to any public fault-finding.[30]

John Grey had his first office in Main Street, where the estates employed a clerk, a bailiff, a moor master, a clerk of ore deliveries and a general inspector of mines.[31] He also lived in Main Street when he arrived in 1832 and spent one early Christmas in 'a vile little parlour at Corbridge'. At Dilston he built a new house for his family of nine (only the youngest, Emily Georgina, was born there – in 1836) but this was not finished until 1835. They regularly attended Corbridge church where he gave all six Grey daughters in marriage and where he, his wife and their daughter-in-law, Emily Mary (1834-64, first wife of Charles Grey who succeeded his father as Receiver and Agent) were buried. He was, however, a great admirer of John Wesley and very sympathetic to the Methodists, for whom he set up a small chapel at Dilston.

Such a powerful figure must have played an important part in the little Corbridge community, most of whom were engaged, in some way, in agriculture, for he showed himself a friend of the farmer, 'a president at their clubs, a judge at their shows and, as far as practical knowledge can go, essentially one of them'[32]. He was the originator of the Tynedale Agricultural Society and of the Hexham Farmers Club. It is likely, too, that he was behind the establishing of Corbridge's first school in 1855, which was built on land belonging to Greenwich Hospital, for he was deeply interested in education and did much to encourage the building of schools.

In the forty years he and his son, Charles, spent at Dilston 'not only visitors but the public generally were allowed to roam at their pleasure over the charming grounds'[33] which had been much improved by the Greys with new walks, lawns, shrubs etc. Charles Grey was a churchwarden during the restoration of the parish church between 1863 and 1867.

The Greenwich Hospital Estates were transferred by the Greenwich Hospital Act of 1865 to the Lords of the Admiralty, by whom the Dilston property was sold to W.B. Beaumont on 12 October 1874, for £132,000.

29. Engraving of Corbridge, 1834

DIRECTORY.

MISCELLANY—Consisting of the Names of the Inhabitants not arranged in the List of Professions and Trades.

Brown John, gentleman, Market place
Brown Mr. Matthew, Water row
Carr John, spirit merchant, Water row
Charlton Mr. Richard Carnaby, Main street
Fairlam Nicholas, clogger, Middle street
Fawcett John, excise officer, Market place
Forster George, cart owner, Watling street
Green Mrs. Mary, Water row
Green Wm. joiner and builder, Water row
Hogarth John, wheelwright, Watling street
Manchester James, gentleman, Princes st.
Nicholson Mrs. Dorothy, Princes street

Richley John, hat manufacturer, assistant overseer, and parish clerk, Watling st.
Riddell Edward, maltster, Main street
Simpson Geo. painter & glazier, Princes st.
Surtees John, circulating library & stationer, Watling street
Surtees William, gentleman, Watling st.
Tweddell George, gentleman, Main street
Walker Bartholomew, lime merchant, Main street
Wilson Rev. George, vicar of Corbridge, Vicarage

LIST OF INHABITANTS—Arranged according to their Professions and Trades.

ACADEMIES.
Crosier Thos. High school
Hewitson Thomas, (subscription) Back row
Jewitt Josiah, Back row
Nicholson Thomas, Main st.

BLACKSMITHS.
Atkin John, Princes street
Bentley Thos. Bridge bank
Forster Ralph, Water row
Knott Stephen, Bridge end

BOOT AND SHOE MAKERS.
Carr John, Water row
Dodd Thomas, Middle st.
Heppell John, Scramblegate
Richley Alfred, Market pl.
Surtees Thomas, Heron's hill

BUTCHERS.
Thompson John, Middle st.
Thompson Wm. Gurner row
Wilkinson John, Middle st.

CORN MILLERS AND FLOUR DEALERS.
*Thus * are Flour Dealers only.*
Lumley Nich. *Manor mill*
*Robson Peter, Heron's hill
*Snowball Thos. Heron's hill

FARMERS.
*Thus * are Yeomen.*
Awburn Thos. *Shawell house*
*Brown John, *Croft house*
*Brown Michael, Main st.
Charlton John and William *Farnleys*
Fairley Wm. *Sheldon house*
Flint George, Main street
Gibson Wm. Stagshaw bank

*Hall Ridley, Main street
Kirsopp Edw. The Hole
*Reed Matthew, Main street
Richley Joseph, Heron's hill
Rochester William, *Linolds*
Thompson Jph. Back row
Watson Wm. *Boggle house*
*Walker Bartw. Main street

GARDENERS.
Bowman Michl. Heron's hill
Falla James, Prier main
Hall Joseph, Princes street
Hall Joseph, Watling street

GROCERS & DRAPERS.
*Thus * are Grocers.*
*Atkinson Wm. Main street
Blandford Thos. (and tallow chandler) Main street
*Dobson Eliz. Water row
Dodd John, Middle street
Dunn Isabella, Gurner row
Hall Joseph, Princes street
Hall Joseph, Watling street
*Harle Thomas, Market pl.
Lumley Bartholomew, Market place
Readhead Tabitha, Water row
*Richley Wm. Scramblegate
Siddell Matthew, Main street
Stokoe Henry, Watling st.
*Surtees Thos. Water row
*Turnbull Edward, Main st.

HOTELS & PUBLIC HOUSES.
Angel Inn, Margaret Blandford, Main street
Boot and Shoe, John Carr, Water row

Golden Fleece, Thos. Thompson, Princes street
Golden Lion, Thos. Surtees, Heron's hill
New Blue Bell, Robt. Hutchinson, Scramblegate
New Inn, George Gibson, Main street
Old Blue Bell, Surtees Forster, Market place
Wheat Sheaf, John Richley, Watling street

MILLINERS & DRESS MAKERS.
Burn Ann, (straw hat mkr.) Middle street
Kirsopp Jane, Princes street
Nicholson Eliz. Main street

STONE MASONS AND BUILDERS.
Atkinson Wm. Main street
Davison Ralph, Watling st.
Forster Surtees, Market pl.
Tate Edward, Prier main

SURGEONS.
Campbell Robt. Watling st.
Lowry George, Water row

TAILORS & DRAPERS.
Atkin Robert, Heron's hill
Hutchinson John, Middle st.
Kirsopp Forster, Watling st.
Kirsopp Geo. Middle street
Smith William, Back row
Soulsby John, Main street
Wood Henry, Scramblegate

WEAVERS & LINEN MFRS.
Hardy Robert, Back row
Turnbull John, Main street

A Wider World

At the end of 1900 a journalist tried to imagine Corbridge as it had been in 1800. 'Descriptions', he wrote, 'are very vague.

From all accounts the village seems to have been in a very bad state, sanitation seems to have been of the worst, small-pox and love being the only things that flourished with any degree of certainty. One writer states that in visiting the town he found that it was very dirty and all the streets except that through which the Newcastle and Carlisle road passed were filthy with middens and pigstyes, and railings before them of split boards etc.[34]

Yet the tough prospered: out of 37 deaths in 1822, 18 were from 60 upwards to 100.

Much of the parish church was still a ruin, as there had been no major repairs for hundreds of years. The east end of the chancel was no more than 'a huge wooden structure'[35]. The Wesleyan Methodists had had a chapel in Back Row since 1820; by the end of the century there would be three flourishing Methodist chapels leading to a certain amount of conflict with the established church. There were several private schools, including schools for the poor, but boys were usually apprenticed from the age of twelve[36]. Agriculture was probably the main occupation for both men and women, and the growing of fruit in market gardens – plums, apples, pears and gooseberries – was becoming important. Many trades and crafts were practised from spinning and weaving – in the 1830s nearly every cottage had a spinning wheel, made from the wood of plum trees – masonry and ironworking to straw-bonnet making. Corbridge was famous for its clogs and shoes, in particular for 'Shields shoes' made for sailors and footwear for lead and coal miners.

A Village of Orchards

From eighty to ninety years ago, regular orchards were formed for the growth of various kinds of apples, pears, gooseberries, etc: the first planted, as far as we can ascertain, was the Croft and Hole orchards; shortly after was planted others by the late father of the present John Bowman, senior…An idea may be formed of the value of such fruit nurseries in favourable seasons, by the produce of one of the half-acre

30. *Parson & White Directory of Durham and Northumberland, 1827*

orchards, situated in Back Row, at the time occupied by a man of the name of William Richley, which realised in one year upwards of £40. The cultivation of the ground for garden produce was soon found to be equally profitable, and its resources became fast developed. On many occasions the value of the onion crop for that season was considered equal to the value of the land on which they were grown....(1881)

Spinning and Weaving

There were thirty pairs of looms which were kept almost constantly at work so that to produce the necessary materials with which to supply the looms, nearly in every cottage and dwelling house was a spinning wheel with which the dame and her daughters were kept plying their fingers, especially during the long winter months, spinning generally twelve cuts to the hank; it was considered one of the essentials of a good wife that she should be a good spinner.[37] (1881)

The Cloggers

In the north of England clogs are still preferred by many farm and factory workers. The warmth and comfort of this form of footwear, coupled with its extraordinary lightness, has many advantages over the rubber Wellington boot which has, in many districts, ousted it from popularity...When clogs were standard footwear...the wearers took great pride in their clogs and used to cut intricate and beautiful patterns in the leather of the 'upper'. This was done with a thin steel instrument, often made from an old umbrella rib. This was sharpened at the end until its edge was sufficiently keen to cut out a fine channel of leather. A paper pattern was then pasted to the leather of the clog and the requisite design cut with the instrument....

The work of making clogs by hand is an extremely difficult operation which calls for great skill. The cutting knives must be guided entirely by the eye of the craftsman who must be able to fashion both soles of a pair to an exact symmetry. There are hardly any young men going into the trade nowadays.[38] (1935)

Rich and Poor

The growing prosperity in the village encouraged builders to buy up old thatched houses and replace them with handsome terraces, and villas were built for the wealthy. Yet there were times of great hardship for the poor, especially in the years before the repeal of the Corn Laws which raised the price of food by keeping

SOUP KITCHEN.

A soup kitchen has been started at the Vicarage, and it is hoped, if the funds permit, to carry it on so long as this severe weather lasts. The distribution of soup will take place every Tuesday and Friday from 10 till 11 A.M., each holder of a ticket being entitled to one quart of soup on payment of a halfpenny. Tickets may be had from Miss Richardson, The Vicarage, or from any of the other district visitors. Gifts of meat, vegetables, etc., will be most welcome, and have already been gratefully received from Messrs. Heslop, Richley, Telfer, and Hamilton. A list of subscriptions received up to date, in aid of the above, is appended :—

	£	s.	d.
The Lady Aline Beaumont	2	0	0
Mrs. Straker	2	0	0
Mrs. Greene	1	1	0
Mr. C. Liddell	1	1	0
Mrs. Watson	0	5	0

C. RICHARDSON.

CORBRIDGE CRICKET CLUB.

The fourth annual concert in connection with the above club was held in the Town Hall, Corbridge, on Tuesday evening, 27th ult. There was a very large and fashionable company present. Great interest was taken in the proceedings, as during the past season the club has won the County Challenge Cup, and the beautiful trophy was unveiled by Lady Aline Beaumont amidst great enthusiasm. The platform was tastefully decorated with plants, &c., and in the background was a nice arrangement of cricketing requisites, bats, wickets, &c. The programme was an excellent one, and each performer was very well received, encores seeming to be the order of the night. Programme :—Orchestral, March ; song, Rothesay Bay, Miss E. Frost ; violin zither solo, Gavotte, Lady Aline Beaumont ; song, The Veteran, Mr A. Foster ; song, Carrier John, Miss Straker ; violin solo, Romance el Sol, Mr Morrison ; song, Yesteryear, Mrs Greene ; comic song, Mr J. Wright ; orchestral, The anvil ; song, One morn a Maiden sought the Mill, Miss Straker ; song, The King and I, Mr A. Foster ; piano duet, The Fairy Queen, The Dowager Lady Londonderry and Lady Aline Beaumont ; song, Fiddle and I, Miss E. Frost ; song, The flight of ages, Mrs Greene ; violin solo, Andante Religioso, Mr Morrison ; comic song, Mr J. Wright. Mrs J. A. Scott played all the accompaniments.

31. Announcement of Soup Kitchen from Parish Magazine, January 1891.

32. Corbridge Cricket Club Annual Concert, announced in Parish Magazine, 1891.

33. Photograph of family of
Rev. Francis Richardson in front of
Vicarage, 1889

Destitute, 1867
*Relief is needed for those who will
not ask for help (to their honour be
it spoken) till every bit of bed and
body-clothing, with any other
portion of their small property, has
been disposed; and those who ask
for help but will not accept it in the
only way it can be given to able-
bodied, viz. in the workhouse[40]*

1880s Agricultural depression
*Many well-dressed and quiet
working people need help for their
households at this time more than
the habitual pauper class, and a
fortnight out of work means empty
cupboards and empty bellies
for many who would scorn to put
themselves on the pauper list of
any church dole.[41]*

out foreign wheat with high
protective taxes. In the 1870s a
succession of wet summers and
bad harvests ruined many farmers,
and those who worked for them
had to rely on the parish dole.

The churchwardens had agreed,
in 1756, to hire a house for
lodging, keeping and employing
the poor of Corbridge. In 1767
they decided that a new Poor
House should be built near the
Wheat Sheaf Inn, at the west end
of what is now Dunkirk Terrace,
on land given in 1706 to the poor
of Corbridge and Halton chapelry
by the will of the then vicar of
Corbridge, Richard Troutbeck[39].
This was a stone, two-storied
building, round a courtyard.
It was dismantled in the 19th
century when the Hexham Union
was built.

General Election

In April 1880 a General
Election aroused fierce passions[42].
The Courant came out strongly
for the Liberal candidates,
Wentworth Beaumont and Albert
Grey, who decided to stand not as
independents, separately soliciting
votes, but as a coalition. Albert
Grey decided to 'fight the battle
on economical principles, by
dispensing with the aid of hired

Corbridge, Northumberland.

conveyances and paid canvassers' –
his expenses in the 1878 election
had been £8000. This time he
would rely on unpaid support. The
Courant devoted three leaders to
the election, commenting that

*every hamlet, we might almost say
every house, is displaying the colours
of the Liberal candidates'.
It is the continuance of the struggle,
ever becoming more and
more intense...which may be said
fairly to have begun when Earl Grey
succeeded in bestowing the franchise
upon the hundreds of thousands*

*who had previously been excluded
from it. It is right and justice
against privilege. It is the claims of
a people against class legislation. It
is economy resisting extravagance,
liberty opposing the growth of
prerogative; in one word, progress
overcoming stagnation[43]*

It was a popular election which
brought Gladstone back to power
with a handsome majority.

NEW TOWN HALL,
CORBRIDGE-ON-TYNE,
Northumberland..

Telegraphic Address ...... Walton, Corbridge.

This magnificent Hall is well-heated with Hot Water
Apparatus, and is brilliantly lighted with a good supply
of Gas from both the ceiling and side-lights, is well-fitted
up and has good Ventilation with fine acoustic properties,
has a Stage or Platform at one end, and a large Gallery
at the other.

Ante-rooms, Cloak-room, Ladies' Lavatory, Gentlemen's
Lavatory, and W.C s.

Two front entrances from the Main Street well-lighted
with Gas, it is quite central and near to Corbridge Railway Station, which is midway between Newcastle and
Carlisle.

This fine Hall will hold about 500, the Charges are
moderate, and Special Rates are quoted for a number of
consecutive nights

For Terms and Vacancies apply to

ISAAC WALTON, Hon Sec.,
CROSS HOUSE, CORBRIDGE.

N.B.—Splendid Accommodation for Tea Parties, Pic-
Nic Parties. The Apparatus is all of the latest improvements. Tea for hundreds can be made in a few minutes.

34. Engraving showing view over garden from workhouse

35. Advertisement for new Town Hall, c.1895.

Rail Travel

The coming of the railway in 1838 brought the first commuters to Corbridge; there were many excursions from the city, and clubs of all kinds, from boating to cycling, became popular.[44] There was fishing and boys would shoot pike between the pillars of the old Roman bridge.[45] Local houses belonging to the gentry, and their gardens – Sandhoe, Stagshaw, Bywell Hall, Styford and Newton Hall and others – were usually open to the public by permission and in the 1880s you could obtain 'terms and arrangements' from Mr J. Summers at the Wheat Sheaf Hotel, Corbridge[46]

It was still a very self-sufficient community, consuming what it produced and relying on its own services. It was also, by our standards, overcrowded. For example, the 1881 census shows 103 people living in Water Row including a family of ten Forsters in no.12. To service this population there were, in 1854, 5 blacksmiths, 17 boot and shoe makers, 4 butchers, 4 cartwrights, 8 gardeners, 12 grocers and dealers in sundries, 3 joiners, 3 painters and 6 tailors and drapers. There were seven inns,

counting the Station Hotel.

From 1863 streets started to be lit by gas, making life much safer for the law-abiding though the subject of lighting was to occupy many parish councils far into the 20th century.

Corbridge in 1881

The village, as it exists at present, is large and well-built, delightfully situated in a beautiful valley on the north bank of the Tyne, on a gentle slope to the south, with its gardens dipping into the river, and is sheltered from the chill blasts of the north by high hills; and on the south at the distance of half a mile, rises a hill of considerable altitude, the sides of which are studded with beautiful villa residences and ordinary dwelling houses...

The absence of all manufactories or anything causing injury to health, the situation of the village, its fine springs of water, its health-giving breezes, its pleasant walks, its nearness to the railway station, all contribute to make it a delightful and enticing resort for visitors in quest of recreation, enjoyment or health.[47]

The Golden Jubilee

In 1887 the Queen celebrated her Golden Jubilee and the country celebrated with her. There was a Great Exhibition in Newcastle and smaller entertainments elsewhere. A subscription list was opened in Corbridge and there were games and tea and a Jubilee mug for 300 children, and 100 poor people were given a knife and fork tea. An appeal to improve the 'lame old'[48] church bells so far exceeded expectations that it was resolved to have a peal of six bells: three old ones were to be recast and three new ones obtained. Mr F.M.Laing of Farnley Grange, who had already obtained land for the new Town Hall, agreed to supply one bell. On 22 April 1888 the new

peal was heard for the first time and a month later the Corbridge Parish Church Guild of Bell-Ringers was formed.[49]

THE BELLS.

On Saturday, March 16th, the additional apparatus to the bells, required for announcing deaths and tolling the funeral knell, was completed. Since the new bells have been hung in the tower the keeping of this ancient custom (which has existed in Corbridge from times immemorial, and still exists in a few other old villages and small towns) has been carried on under exceptional difficulties and dangers. Now, by the addition of this apparatus, all difficulty and danger is removed. In future the death announcements will be as follows :—

3 years old and under,	3	strokes on Nos.	3, 4, 5	bells,	3	times.	
4 years to 17 years old,	5	,,	3, 4, 5	,,	3	,,	
18 & upwards, unmarried,	7	,,	3, 4, 5	,,	3	,,	
18 ,, married,	9	,,	3, 4, 5	,,	3	,,	

And the age on the large or tenor bell. For funerals the large bell will be tolled every half minute.

36. Revival of custom of tolling the funeral bell. Parish Magazine, 1889

37. The Corbridge Bell-Ringers Guild,
c.1900. Includes Bob Douglas,
Harry Nesbit, Billy Arkless.
Jack Davison, Bob Richley

Letter from Hotel,
Salt Lake City, (1901)

Dear Sir,
Will you kindly give me any information regarding the family of John Jamison, formerly of Prior Mains, Corbridge, my uncle and my mother's brother?

On September 14, 1852, we left Corbridge for Canada, where my father, Matthew Maddison, and my mother, Nancy Maddison, both died, the former in 1877 and the latter in 1884... Years have not dulled my memory of the old village with its crooked streets, its 'pants' and wells, and the river where I so often waded and bathed and caught the crowding minnows with a pin-hole. The old place and its surroundings are an open book after all these years...

I may even now be writing to one whose father played with me at 'Kitty cat and buck stick' in childhood or who sat on the same form with me at school or played 'high spy' in the mellowy light of the moon on summer nights in company.

(signed) **Matthew Maddison**[51]

Cycling

The most enjoyable outing of the season was to Corbridge...Gliding past some attractive residences, the descent to the village was made, legs over handles and all speed on, the wind getting a grand hold on us and tempting us to take an involuntary plunge into the clear water below. Just as the clock stood at seven so the machines were stabled in the Market Place and the adjacent Temperance Hotel was the scene of hasty ablutions... A splendid tea followed and with lilies adorning their manly breasts the sunburned riders strolled by the river or sought out antiquated places of interest.[50]

ESTABLISHED 1838.

:o:

M. ELLERINGTON,

(Successor to the late R. FORSTER),

PRACTICAL WATCH & CLOCK MAKER,

CORBRIDGE,

Begs most respectfully to thank his numerous customers for the kind patronage he has received during the 10 years that he has carried on business, and would also intimate that all orders in future will receive his best attention.

ELECTRO-PLATED GOODS

OF BEST QUALITY.

Pianos, Harmoniums, American Organs,

(New and Second-Hand) for sale or hire.

Spectacles and Eye Glasses to suit all Sights.

TABLE and POCKET CUTLERY

Of the leading Sheffield Makers.

Writing Desks, Work Boxes, Jewel Cases, and Ladies' Companions.

Looking Glasses and Ladies' Hand Glasses.

ANEROIDS' BAROMETERS IN STOCK

Other Makers to order.

A large Stock of Walking Sticks always on hand.

AGENT FOR

Sewing, Wringing and Washing Machines.

☞ For particulars of the various departments in my business see the other side.

INDIA AND CHINA TEA WAREHOUSE,

Market Place, Corbridge.

EDWARD HESLOP,

FAMILY GROCER,

Tea, Coffee and Spice Merchant,

CHEESE, BUTTER & BACON FACTOR.

Dealer in Flour and Feeding Meals.

Respectfully tenders thanks to the public for their liberal support and trusts by continuing to supply Goods of the

VERY BEST QUALITY

AT THE

Lowest Remunerative Prices,

To receive a further share of their patronage

E. H. wishes to notify that since removing to larger premises he is able to Stock heavy when the Markets are at the lowest point, and his customers shall have the benefit accordingly.

E. H. begs to state that his usual Stock is over

1500 Pounds of TEA,

and are procured from the best Markets for cash, and are carefully blended on the premises.

All Goods are delivered on the shortest notice.

V.   R.

CORBRIDGE POST OFFICE

REGULATIONS.

This Office is opened on Week Days at 7 a.m., and is closed at 8 p.m. Sundays it is open from 8 to 10 a.m.

DESPATCHES

Letters and Parcels are despatched at 9-20 a.m.

Do.   do.   11-15 a.m.

Do.   do.   3-30 p.m.

Do.   do.   7-45 p.m.

Sundays: Letters only do   7-0 a.m.

Delivery of Letters, &c., commences at 7-45 a.m., 3-45 p.m., and 6-45 pm. Sundays 8-45 to 10 a.m. (Callers only.)

Money Order, Postal Order, Savings Bank Business transacted. Inland Revenue Licenses issued, on Week Days from 9 a.m. to 6 p.m., and on Saturdays to 8 p.m. Telegraph Business is transacted on Week Days from 8 a.m. to 8 p.m. ; and on Sundays from 8 to 10 a.m.

Inland Parcel Post.

Parcels are received for transmission from 1 lb. to 11 lb. weight, and charged 3d. for the first 1 lb., and 1½d. for every additional lb.

Particulars of Foreign and Colonial Parcel Post may be obtained at the Office

The dimensions allowed for an Inland Postal Parcel will be :—

Maximum length   ...   3 ft. 6 in.

Maximum length and gerth combined   6 ft. 0 in.

H. DODD, POSTMISTRESS.

38. Trade advertisements, from M. Ellerington, *Brief History and Guide of Corbridge, c.1886*

39. Church tower and clock, c.1880, showing 18th-century clock

40. Jubilee clock, installed 1897. Photo, c.1970

The Diamond Jubilee

The new Town Hall was opened in the summer of 1887: at last the village had a really handsome centre for meetings, dances, bazaars and all kinds of celebration. And by the end of the century Corbridge had a parish council (1895), established under the Local Government Act of 1894. Two years later, in 1897, the village celebrated the Queen's Diamond Jubilee by installing a new clock in the church tower to replace the one that had served the village since 1767[52], at a total cost of £131 16s.

The Starting of the Jubilee Clock

A temporary platform was erected at the north end of the Market Place for the ceremony... The Chairman (Mr D. Stephens) of the Jubilee Celebration Committee said they had assembled to witness the opening of the new Jubilee Clock by Mrs J.H.Straker who had kindly consented to perform that ceremony... The Vicar addressed the large audience and stated there had been two or three movements made to get a new clock erected in the tower of the church, but it was not until last Easter Vestry that it took a practical form, as subscriptions

were then promised towards purchasing a clock as a memorial for that Jubilee year... The Chairman asked Mrs Straker kindly to start the clock, and by pulling a string that lady set the Jubilee clock in the old tower of St Andrews a-going, and about a minute after that performance it chimed the half hour, it being then half-past-two o'clock. We may add that the new clock has two dials, with ding-dong quarters and striking hours[53].

But when did the century end? There was much discussion, majority opinion decreeing that this was at the end of 1900.

*Another 100 years have gone and we've seen a century's close
What the present may bring forth I can't tell as you'll suppose
One thing's certain, we'll not be here to take offence
When they jeer at our antique methods in another century hence*

*Will our roads be paved with wood and some decent seats erected?
Will there be a public park or perhaps we can't expect it.
Will there be a side walk across the bridge if we stump up all our pence?
Will the station footpath be asphalted in another century hence?[54]*

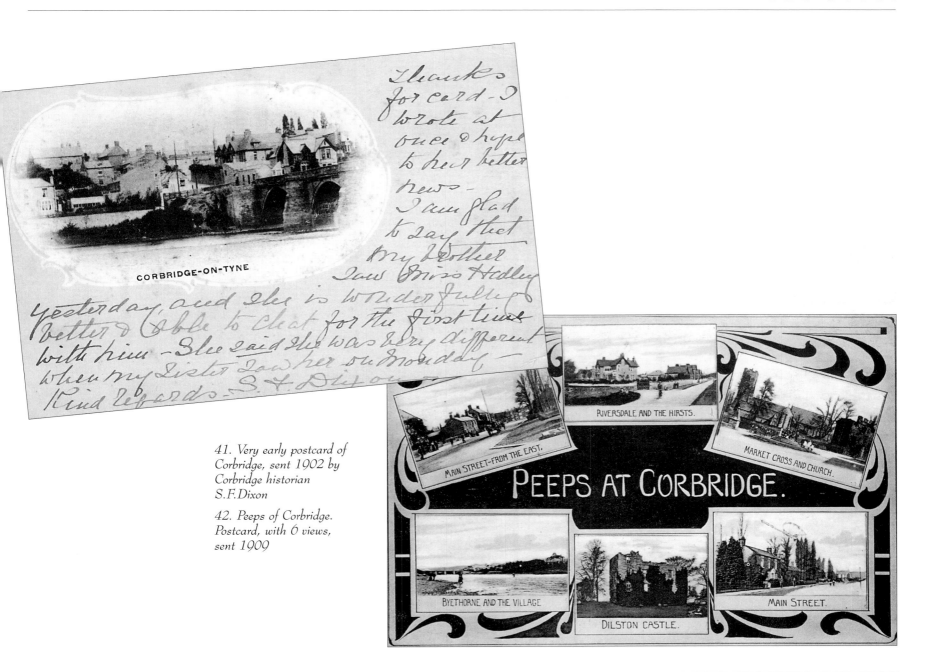

CORBRIDGE-ON-TYNE

Thanks for card – I wrote at once & hope to hear better news – I am glad to say that my brother saw Miss Hedley yesterday and she is wonderfully better & able to chat for the first time with him – She said she was very different when my Sister saw her on Monday – Kind regards – S. F. Dixon

41. Very early postcard of Corbridge, sent 1902 by Corbridge historian S.F.Dixon

42. Peeps of Corbridge. Postcard, with 6 views, sent 1909

PEEPS AT CORBRIDGE.

MAIN STREET-FROM THE EAST.

RIVERSDALE AND THE HIRSTS.

MARKET CROSS AND CHURCH.

BYETHORNE AND THE VILLAGE

DILSTON CASTLE.

MAIN STREET.

A Century of Wars

Boer War

In 1900 England was involved in an immensely expensive war against the Boers of the Transvaal who, under the leadership of Paul Kruger and supported by Germany, proved hard to defeat. For 217 days a British garrison of 700 under the command of Colonel Baden-Powell was besieged by the Boers in the town of Mafeking in the northern Cape. The siege ended on 17 May 1900 and the country went wild.

The Relief of Mafeking

was celebrated throughout the country, not least in Corbridge.

The bells of the parish church rang and rockets and guns were fired and crowds paraded the streets singing loyal and patriotic songs. In the evening tea was given in the Town Hall. The proceedings opened with the National Anthem and afterwards a procession was formed. First came the band of the (Corbridge) Company of the 1st Volunteer Battalion of the Northumberland Fusiliers, St Andrews (Corbridge) Co. of

43. Celebration in Town Hall, c.1910, perhaps Coronation of George V
44. Corbridge Church Choir, c.1909

the Church Lads Brigade, then members of the Corbridge Cycling Club, their machines being decorated with Chinese lanterns followed by a huge crowd who marched round the village carrying an effigy of Kruger. A halt was made in the Market Place where the latter was burnt, amid ringing cheers[55].

And there were further celebrations for the **return of the volunteers**:

*Corbridge was en fête for the coming home from the Boer War of volunteers who had gone 15 months ago with the Service Company... The inhabitants had vied with themselves in the display of bunting etc., and the result was that the place was decorated beyond all expectations. Streamers and long lines of banneretts were fluttering from nearly every window and on the end of the bridge a triumphal arch had been erected with the words across the top '**Welcome Home**'. At last the bugle sounded and there was the biggest muster of volunteers I had seen for some considerable time... To the tune of a stirring march, the cavalcade made its way to the station, the rear of the procession being brought up by a gaily decorated brake.[56]*

Boer War Trophies

There is on view in Mr Forster's shop in Middle Street, some interesting curios from the seat of war sent by Mr T.C.Forster who, as my readers will be aware, went out with the A and B Companies of the Northumberland Yeomanry. Corporal Forster, who was one of the best shots in the regiment, was one of the first to volunteer. Among the interesting objects are: an ostrich egg; 'The Mafeking Mail'; some Kruger coins; a Pom-Pom shell; some poisoned cartridges found in the Boer trenches; and a card presumably circulated amongst the troops as a memento of the annexation of the Transvaal and Free States[57].

45. Gardeners' outing to Lake District, c.1905

46, 47. Advertisements from Corbridge Parish Magazine, March 1909 (continued on pp.42, 43 and 56)

Death of the Queen

A year later, in 1901, the old Queen died and a muffled peal was rung in Corbridge church by members of the bell-ringers' guild: Messrs J.Davison, W.Arkless, C.Gardner, H.Davison, H.Nesbitt, D.Wilson and W.Ward. The altar was draped in black. As the new King was proclaimed, it was remembered that 'there is at present living in the village an old woman, Mrs Allcroft, who has lived under the regime of four monarchs: George III, William IV, Queen Victoria and Edward VII'[58].

The War to End Wars

The 1914 war started with the enthusiasm of countless volunteers whose deaths, over the next few years, chronicled with photographs in the *Hexham Courant*, were to touch almost every family. Much pressure was put on the young men for there was no conscription until 1916.

In a memorable scene at the Coigns a large and enthusiastic meeting was presided over by Major Hedley who told them that much depended upon the young men and they should join the Army now. In Corbridge, he was pleased to say, their company, the 'E' Company of the 4th Battalion Northumberland

Fusiliers, one of the finest in the county, was now at full strength. Out of 92 men, 87 had volunteered immediately for Imperial Service[59]

'Corbridge to Be Prepared'

On Saturday 15 August, eleven days after the declaration of war, a Vigilance and Investigation Committee was set up 'for the consideration of rendering the necessary relief and protection of the residents of the district'. It would collect funds for wives and dependents of volunteers; keep a register of men available; and organize and equip a band of special constables in case it became necessary to control food supplies. But, the Rev. Henderson-Kay asked, 'Are we allowed to do this? Have we received any special powers?'

They hadn't, but feelings were running high. It was thought that profiteers were trying to corner the wheat and potato crops. Major Hedley told a meeting, 'He was not very vindictive but to anyone

48. *Church Lads Brigade, 1910.*   49. *Soldiers, 1916. Donald Hall is 1st on left in 3rd row*

HEXHAM RURAL NATIONAL SERVICE COMMITTEE.

This Committee has been appointed to canvass the Rural District, with the view of obtaining Volunteers for National Service.

The object of National Service is to get all men between the ages of 18 and 61 (in whatever occupation they may be employed, including Agriculture) to enrol as National Service Volunteers, and to place themselves at the disposal of the Director General of National Service during the War, so that they may be put, if it becomes necessary, to any employment in which workers may, in the interests of the nation, at the time be required, on the understanding that, as far as national requirements admit, Volunteers will be engaged in their own locality upon the work for which they are best fitted.

The canvass is to be completed by the end of this month, and the Committee think that the work could be best and most expeditiously carried through if the Parish Councils, where there are Parish Councils, and the Parish Meetings, where there are not Parish Councils, would undertake to arrange with volunteers to canvass their respective Parishes.

The details as to the nature of the canvass have not yet been received; but the Committee feel that, in view of the short time left for carrying through the work, arrangements should be made at once, so that the canvass may be started without delay as soon as the requisite instructions are received.

With this object, I have to ask you to submit this matter to your Parish Council, or Parish Meeting, as the case may be, at the earliest possible moment, and to express the earnest hope of this Committee that they will undertake this work, which at the present time is of supreme national importance. I shall be glad to know as soon as possible what decision is arrived at by your Parish Council, or Parish Meeting; and, if it is decided to undertake the work, what number of Canvassers they propose to employ, and, approximately, how many men between the ages of 18 and 61 they anticipate there will be in the parish, in order that I may have some idea of the forms required.

Information as to the terms and conditions of employment where a man is called up for service is given on the Enrolment Form, of which I enclose a copy, and which can be obtained at any Post Office.

It was also suggested that very material assistance could be given to the movement by explaining it at your Annual Parish Meeting.

50. Appeal for volunteers, 1916

51. Peace Day party for school children, 19 July 1919

who was mean enough to make a profit out of the toil and trouble of his country he would say they ought to be hung and he would help to do it'[60].

Mrs Pumphrey of Hindley Hall, addressing a society for Women's Suffrage, advised girls of spirit who were thinking of getting married to prefer perpetual maidenhood rather than marry a slacker. Under the present system, the best men went to the front and slackers stayed behind to be fathers of the next generation.[61]

Shirts, Socks & Sandbags

Gifts of shirts and socks were received by Mrs Hedley of Gresham House and in 1915 Dilston Hall was equipped as a hospital for the wounded. There were instructions how to make badly-needed sandbags for the trenches, and appeals to subscribe to the War Loan. By October 1915 Hexham War Hospital Supply and Clothing Depot had supplied 4538 swabs, 709 bandages, 92 pairs of slippers and 1705 other garments. In 1916 the Government was under great pressure to supply ever more men, though they were inexperienced

and untrained, to relieve the French at Verdun, and the result was the terrible battle of the Somme when 57,000 British soldiers were killed in a few hours.

Victory, when it came, was celebrated quietly: too much had been lost.

Afterwards

Memorials were built to commemorate the dead. 1920 saw the first Armistice Day, with two minutes' silence at the time fighting ended on the eleventh hour of the eleventh day of the eleventh month. At the entrance to the church, a lych gate was erected to remember the 109 Corbridge soldiers who had died fighting. Initiatives, stalled because of the war, restarted. A new Cottage Hospital building, discussed in 1913, was opened in 1918. The Corbridge branch of the Women's Institute was founded in 1918; it was an immediate success and after the war it grew rapidly.

Leisure Between the Wars

The period between the wars was one of increasing prosperity and leisure for many. In summer there were boating and cycling clubs, tennis, cricket, fishing, walks beside the river; and, in 1929, Corbridge got its own golf club and players no longer had to climb a steep hill to the course above Riding Mill. Corbridge had long been a popular resort but the preparation of a village guide book in 1918, to encourage visitors, had a rather cynical reception from the *Courant*'s Corbridge reporter. 'Let us', he wrote, 'put our strawberries on top of our basket and keep sewerage and river pollution and our dangerous electrification poles and so on far away from public gaze.'

In winter the Town Hall was filled almost every night with activities of various kinds, all advertised by posters stuck on walls and doors by the bill-poster. Concerts, often by distinguished performers, and lectures, particularly travel talks illustrated with lantern slides, were immensely popular. There were charity bazaars and dances, all involving a lot of work in decoration and flower-arranging, and a great deal of money was raised for those suffering from long years of unemployment, especially the miners.

52. Minute of meeting to establish Women's Institute in Corbridge, 13 March 1918

53. *John Bishop with his wife Ellen and elder son, John Cecil, outside cottage at Howden Dene,*

54. *John Bishop in his 1903 Maudsley, 20hp driving the rear wheels through a 4-speed gearbox and double chain drive. The passenger is William Charles Hornsby (Willie the Jock) who rode in the Blaydon Races*

Quoits was very popular: at one time Corbridge had four teams, one of which was at the Golden Lion.

Corbridge had the oldest soccer club in the north, founded in the 1870s. There was rugby football and hockey and, above all, the excitement of riding in a motor car. In 1921 John Bishop opened his new workshop in Main Street. It was equipped with machinery for manufacturing scarce spare parts and in 1922 the first petrol pumps in Northumberland were installed at Corbridge and Wideopen.

Cars for Corbridge

John Bishop (1879-1939) was a pioneer motorist. Born into a Herefordshire farming family, he had always been fascinated by machines. He left home when he was fourteen, and eventually found work with Cyril Maudsley, an early car manufacturer. In 1903 he was asked to deliver a Maudsley to Beaufront Castle, Northumberland, for Captain

J.H.Cuthbert, DSO and his wife, who had just returned from their honeymoon. As the coachman couldn't manage the 'horseless carriage' Bishop was asked to stay.

In 1920, Lady Rayleigh, the widow of Captain Cuthbert who had been killed in the war, lent Bishop £1000 to start his own business in Main Street, Corbridge, as a motor engineer and agent. He drove the Duke of Gloucester, then Prince Henry, to open the Hexham War Memorial Hospital; was the first person to drive a car to Hexham Race Course; and had,

among his notable customers, (he also had a taxi service) Lord Baden-

55. *Postcard, with 6 views of Corbridge inside, sent to Miss C. Buddle, PO Hebburn Colliery, 1922*

56. Church of England Sunday School concert, 1925, produced by Miss Nicholson (centre back) in new Parish Hall.

57. Boating Green showing Boating Hut, c.1920

13. CORBRIDGE FROM BOATING GREEN.

Powell, the Duchess of Bedford and Rudyard Kipling.

In 1934 Bishop took his elder son, John Cecil, into partnership; later his other son, Stephen Bishop, joined his brother as a partner.[62] The business became a limited company in 1956 and remained a Rover franchise until 1999. It still operates in Corbridge.

Carr's garage, which eventually occupied most of the ground floor of the Town Hall, had a similar history: Carr had been a chauffeur at Stagshaw House.

58. Butterfly Queen, performed by C. of E. Sunday School in Parish Hall, c.1925

59. *Empire Day c.1925, celebrated on 24 May, Queen Victoria's birthday*

A kiss of the sun for pardon,
The song of the birds for mirth;
You are nearer God's heart in a garden,
Than anywhere else on earth.

THE ORCHARD
Pleasure Park and Tea Gardens.

Large Open Spaces for Sports, Sunday School Trips, Cycling Clubs and Staff Outings catered for. The Orchard is stocked with Fruit Trees. There is a Maze, also Quoit Pitches. Large Open Spaces for Games & other Amusements Hard Tennis Court. Ample Covered Accommodation for a wet day. An Ideal place for Campers.

FURTHER INFORMATION FROM:
BRIDGE BANK,
CORBRIDGE-ON-TYNE.
Telephone .... 34 Corbridge.

1928.

With the Compliments of
THE PROPRIETOR,
THE ORCHARD PLEASURE PARK AND TEA GARDENS,
CORBRIDGE-ON-TYNE.

60. Rowing Club, 1910

63. Tennis Club, c.1910

61. Calendar of Events 1928, with advertisement from Orchard Pleasure Park and Gardens

62. C. of E. Country Dance Team, c.1924

Another War

But for many the '30s were a very grim time. The 'war to end wars' had not brought prosperity and many of those who fought in it returned to unemployment and dreadful housing conditions. When, on 3 September 1939, it was announced that the nation was at war, few had any illusions about what this meant: memories of the 1914-18 war were still vivid. That Christmas King George V1 made the first wartime broadcast to the Empire to an audience of 150 million, and the Corbridge Choral Society (who each year sang carols at Roecliff Lodge) was invited to take part.

Corbridge Carol Singers in Empire Link-Up Christmas Day Broadcast

Each item in the Christmas Day broadcast is a carefully polished gem, and Corbridge Carol singers are seeing to it that the high standard set in their broadcast last Christmas Eve of Christmas carols in a traditional setting...will be fully maintained, if not surpassed... In the panelled hall at Roecliff, the firelight playing hide-and-seek among the Cromwellian armours and the coach horns with which the walls

are hung, the carol singers will be waiting to offer their three minutes contribution to the programme.

Accompanying the choir with the liquid notes of Northumbrian pipes will be the well-known Northumbrian piper, Mr Jack Armstrong. Listeners will hear the Master of the House, 84-year-old Mr J.T.Mail, extend a welcome to the singers and the greetings being amplified by his son, the well-known naturalist, Mr Percy Mail.

The Corbridge Carol singers, under their leader Miss S.Hall, have been singing carols in the traditional manner for almost 30 years...After the performance the candle lamps would be snuffed and members of the choir would pair up for a long walk to the next 'pitch'. Rumour has it that quite a number of matrimonial matches were struck as the result of these carolling jaunts.[03]

Rationing and the Black-Out

For civilians in Corbridge, as elsewhere, war meant anxiety, restrictions and deprivation, though also a sense of community arising from the feeling that we were all in it together, and a new public interest in the health of the children. People were exhorted to save by buying Savings Certificates; to take fewer and smaller baths; to salvage everything 'from flat irons to two-ton boilers'; to save paper; to collect sheep's wool off the barbed wire in the fields; to gather rose-hips to provide vitamins for children. The newspapers shrank in size and were filled with suggestions about how to keep warm or make palatable meals with powdered egg and Spam. Young women joined the forces or made munitions; those who remained at home sewed and knitted for the troops or became landgirls.

Corbridge became a garrison town. Soldiers were billeted in any unused or underused buildings, or

64. *Look Out in the Black-Out. Wartime Railway Poster*

in private houses. The officers' mess was in Colwyn, in St Helen's Lane; the sergeants' mess in the house now occupied by the optometrist in Hill Street. Gresham House, in Watling Street, became a hospital and the ambulances were kept at Springfield Mews in Main Street.

The Pele tower was used as a report centre for the ARP (Air Raid Protection) service and

Corbridge created an air-raid shelter in a Roman building at Corstopitum.

A Roman Shelter

A few months ago a strongly-built underground treasure chamber was unearthed - a good solid structure with stone steps leading down to it. A new timber roof, covered with sods of earth, has been added, and an excellent dug-out has resulted.[64]

In December 1940 Corbridge sent 200 Christmas parcels to the troops, costing 10s (50p) each and made up in the Oddfellows Hall[65] in Watling Street. Each parcel contained a 2lb. fruit loaf, 50 cigarettes, 2 slabs of chocolate, a packet of biscuits, and a pair of hand-knitted socks or helmet. A 12-year-old boy, Matthew Bell, sent the muffler he had knitted.

Iron Railings for the Melting Pot

In September 1941 it was announced that iron railings, with few exceptions, must be melted down for munitions. There was a heated debate in a parish council meeting. Mr Pigg said 'He was strongly opposed to cemetery

65. *Home Guard, 1940.*

66. *Railings at Greencroft Avenue, 1909, removed in 1941/2*

railings and iron work round graves being interfered with'. To which the answer was, 'If it made the difference between victory and defeat, they should go'. Mr Pegg, another councillor, added that he had sacrificed a large part of his library to the war effort.[66]

In the end, almost all Corbridge's railings were surrendered voluntarily, including some beautiful ones in Greencroft Avenue. But the metal was never used for munitions.

Helpful Hint

To warm a bedroom, light a candle and set it in a flower pot, then turn another flower pot the same size upside down over it. This makes a perfect stove as the clay pot holds and radiates the heat. It should be going two hours or more before one retires. It is invaluable to those who have a cough, as the warmed air soothes the chest[67].

The Black-Out, which was rigorously enforced, restricted social life: to walk through the unlit streets in winter was a perilous undertaking as was driving with masked lights. People stayed at home and the wireless became all-important. A Corbridge woman was fined for accidentally turning on the light on the landing when she went to her baby and many others were prosecuted. Rationing, which started in January 1940, continued until 1954. Bread was rationed for the first time in 1946, a year after the war ended. It was grey and rather nasty and to begin with bakers were left with shelves of stale bridge as housewives saved their rations.

The use of hand torches by pedestrians will be permitted subject to the following conditions. The light must be dimmed by placing two sheets of tissue paper or its equivalent over the glass bulb or the aperture through which the light is emitted. The light from the torch must at all times be projected downwards. All torches must be extinguished during the period of an air-raid warning[08].

Evacuees

There were two very cold winters in 1940 and 1947, followed in each case by floods. Corbridge became an evacuee centre, almost doubling its population by 1940; and there were many tensions as children from very different backgrounds learned about each

other. Schools were overcrowded—there were two shifts for lessons – and the golf club, one of the most popular forms of entertainment, prospered. Local farmers were allocated Italian or German prisoners-of-war from camps at

Aydon or Featherstone Castle.

Silencing of the Bells

To the annoyance of the Vicar, the Rev. M. Barlow, the church bells were silenced as a security measure in September 1940 (bells were to

be rung only if there was an invasion or parachute landing) when he was on holiday though Mr Pigg, a councillor, protested that 'Big Ben is still striking'. There was a real fear of invasion and the bridge was defended by two enormous cement blocks (to impede tanks). There were more cement blocks in Princes Street.

Victory Celebrations

On VE (Victory in Europe) Day, 8 May 1945, there was a service round the Market Cross conducted by the Vicar, and evening services in the parish church and the Methodist church in Princes Street. There was a bonfire on the Boating Green.

VJ Day (Victory in Japan, the real end to the war) was celebrated on Wednesday 14 August 1945. Bonfires were lit and there were fireworks. Every street arranged a party for the children, each of whom was given fruit, chocolate and a threepenny piece. In Front Street and Market Street the tables were decorated with red, white and blue and the cakes were iced with 'patriotic colours'.

67. Carnival, Corbridge, c.1945

A Cold Dark Year

The National Health service set up by the new Labour government brought many changes but the Charlotte Straker hospital continued as before and in 1947 received the accolade that it was performing a 'very necessary service'. But otherwise 1947 started miserably: 125 colliers were storm-bound in the Tyne and domestic heating by electricity was forbidden between 9am and noon and 2 to 4pm. There was a ban on greyhound racing, suspension of the BBC Third programme[69] and in Corbridge the number of street lights was reduced. In March the Parish Council decided that in view of the crisis there would be no more lighting that winter. There was heavy rain in late summer, spoiling the harvest. 1947 became the worst year in living memory for farmers.

It was in this grim year that a remarkable institution of Corbridge life was born. Jean Hickleton was persuaded by two ladies in their eighties, the Misses Thompson, to take over their shop in Middle Street, previously the premises of Mr Snowball, tailor,

and before that of Mrs Pearson. It is now part of Norma James.

A Fashionable Foundation

'Jean' sold clothes for men, women and children, as well as wool and haberdashery, all under one roof until 1954 when she opened a new

shop for wools and children's wear in Front Street and, in 1962, a 'children's only' shop in Watling Street. 'She prided herself on being able to supply every requisite for the home dressmaker, as well as all embroidery and knitting requirements'. The wool shop stocked 1/2 ton of knitting wool.

Jean was also known for the excellence of her corsetry. Most of the staff had certificates for corsetry fitting, for Mrs Hickleton, in common with her customers, believed than 'every woman is entitled to a good, properly fitted foundation garment. A good foundation is still the basis of a good appearance'.

Interview with Jean Hickleton

She recalls that in the 1950s she used to take delivery of one dozen pairs of nylons for every three dozen pairs of lisle. She said, 'I used to have a quota system for my customers. I wrote their names in a little book and if they bought three pairs of lisles they were entitled to a pair of nylons. They were in such short supply this was the only way to be fair'. (1972)[70]

There was a desperate shortage of houses and in March 1950 there were 200 on the waiting list for Corbridge Council houses, 'some of them living in deplorable conditions'. Two of these precious houses were allocated to men living outside the area but on the Council payroll and there was a public outcry.[71] There was a plague of rabbits – still a staple food – made worse for the farmers by the flooding of the market with frozen Australian rabbits.

A Nurse's annexe was opened at the Cottage Hospital in 1950 as a memorial to Dr Noel Jackson, founder of the extremely successful Corbridge branch of the **Red Cross**, and founding member of the **Golf Club**. The Corbridge roundabout was finished just in time for the first County Show ever to have been held in the village in August 1950. On the 35-acre site there were five acres of trade stalls with 1043 stock entries, including 86 for 'heavy' horses, and 507 industrial entries[72].

The Coronation

In February 1952, the country learned 'with shocked amazement' that King George VI, who had shared their hardship during the war and after, had died. In Corbridge the cinema was closed and the shops were draped in black. The following year, on 5 June, the young Queen Elizabeth was crowned amid great excitement: this, it was felt, was the beginning of a new age. But it was November weather, cold and wet: in Corbridge it didn't stop raining until the evening when bonfires were lit on Prospect Hill.

On the great day itself, the Coronation Committee got through the bulk of its heavy programme of celebrations...Mrs Wilson of Springfield Cottages and Mrs Little of 5, St Helen's Lane were judged to have the best decorated houses in the village. Mrs Gordon

(confectioner) of Princes Street, took first prize for business premises, Mr Wm Merkin[73] (fruiterer) of Market Place and Mr G. Robson (ironmonger) of Middle Street being awarded second and third prizes...Best decorated licensed premises were the Wheatsheaf and

the Black Bull hotels...The fancy dress parade was held in the Drill Hall and there were many topical and amusing costumes. Triumphant Everest mountaineers, newly knighted Gordon Richards and Jack Hobbs – even the changeable British weather – were all there.[74]

Floods

Two years later, in the spring of 1955, Corbridge experienced its worst flood since 1881. The river rose ten feet in four hours. Seventeen houses were flooded; six newborn babies and their mothers had to be evacuated from the

68. (opposite) Part of Norma James. She bought Jean's shop in Middle Street in 1970.

69. Station Hotel isolated by floods, 10 December 1955

70. Ken and Frank Soulsby and Bill Henderson launching boat to ferry residents to safety, December 1955
71. Flooding in Station Road, 10 December 1955

72. (opposite) TynedaleAgricultural Show, August 1948. Roland Robinson with Cocklaw Heather and Baroness

windows of the Maternity Hospital; and there was severe damage to the cemetery. Firemen and police climbed ladders to the windows of houses to feed the villagers. Business men, arriving from Newcastle at the station, were told: 'Your village is divided, there is no way to houses on the north bank'. They had to travel on to Hexham, returning by a special bus service.

A Corbridge farmer went back forty years to keep up-to-date on Monday night. When floods cut electricity supplies to the village and put his all-mains radio out of action, he tuned into the BBC's news bulletins on a crystal set.[75]

Agricultural Show

Yet in August that year Corbridge proudly became 'the Bank Holiday Mecca of the North' again, making agricultural history by being the first village to stage two County Shows in five years. Only a few months ago there had been a seven-foot lake; now there was a 'town' of agricultural stands. Among the crowd of 35,000, the *Courant* reported, were 'shipyard workers, miners, office clerks and

city typists seeking to rub shoulders with shepherds from the hills and ploughmen from the valleys'.

Saved from 'Squalid Suburbia'

1965 saw the creation of the Corbridge Village Trust. Dr T.Hird talked of the 'fear of squalid suburbia' as planning permission

was given for the 17 acres of the Crofts estate at the east end of the village. There would be 144 houses with flat roofs and castellated edges, to be built, so the planners insisted, in a 'mellow grey brick evocative of the

sandstone of the village'. They would cost between £400 and £1000 each. Mr Roland Cookson, of Howden Dene and owner of the land, explained that he had been persuaded to sell because of the need for high-class housing for those working in industry in the north-east, and that he was strongly opposed to low-standard houses. With the assistance of members of the Trust, the plans were rejected and a new scheme submitted.

The Village in the 1970s

In 1974, the Village Trust invited students of Newcastle University's School of Architecture to report on the visual appearance of the village. The population was then just over 3,000. Several properties at that time were empty and the village was peppered with traffic signs, with three in Hill Street. The students also drew attention to the tangle of overhead wires at the north end of Watling Street, (removed only at the end of 1999) and the prominent 'Toilet' sign perched on top of the Market Cross.

In their introduction to the *Corbridge Improvement Project* the students said that the village supports 'enough shops to provide residents with all essential goods..but Hexham can offer a far wider choice of goods and Corbridge has little to attract shoppers from the surrounding rural areas'. That this has changed owes a lot to the new village businesses of the 1970s and later, notably Norma James, the Forum bookshop, Richard Burt's Corbridge Larder, and the Corbridge branch of Waltons which has outlasted its parent in Hexham. The Town Hall buildings are once again fully used: they accommodate a number of successful traders, including that mainstay of village life, the pharmacy of Martin Merriman.[76]

Corbridge did, however, acquire a new library in April 1976 and 1600 books were taken out on the first day.

Saving the Charlotte Straker

The great village achievement between 1985 and 1992 was the saving of the Charlotte Straker hospital. When its closure was announced in 1988, powerful local opposition, brilliantly coordinated by Dr Graham Grant, Dr Bill Cunningham and many other villagers, resulted in the setting up of the Charlotte Straker Project Trust. Mrs Catherine Cookson, Patron of the Trust, who had lived in Corbridge for many years previously, started the fund-raising with a donation of £25,000; and an anonymous donor gave £100,000. The result was the opening in 1992, the date of the proposed closure, of a newly-equipped hospital, with bed-sitting rooms, flats and bungalows for the elderly.

The Chains

A sadder decision was confirmed in June, 2000. This concerns the Chains, on land belonging to the Duke of Northumberland and granted by him in 1849 'to the use of cottagers in the village for spade cultivation, at a moderate charge'. The land is between St Helen's Street and St Helen's Lane, and is the site of the second manor hall and St Helens's chapel, built after the Scottish raid of 1296.

At a public inquiry into the new Local Plan, the Inspector ruled that the Chains was the appropriate site for the fifty houses allocated to Corbridge. Although this was the only option that could prevent additional traffic congestion, as new residents will not need to drive to shops, it will mean an end to the allotments, and there is lot of local opposition to yet more building in Corbridge.

Corbridge is a village with a fascinating history whose identity our planners should be concerned to preserve. Yet the scale and quality of development has been unsympathetic and has damaged its unique character. In 1975 Walter Iley[77] wrote that 'population increase on the recent scale is unnecessary and unwise, and could go far to destroy the village'. How much more is this true in 2000.

73. Advertisement, 1909

Around Corbridge

The Bridge

Et Corabrige, the name by which our village is first mentioned in the Northumbrian Annals, means 'at the Cora bridge' It is thus one of the very few pre-Conquest place names (Cambridge and Stamfordbridge are others) whose names come from the word 'bridge'. Corbridge became important as a trading centre because of the bridge which carried Dere Street across the Tyne at the point where it crossed the Stanegate.

But by the 13th century the Roman bridge was certainly no longer usable though traces of it remained above water until the late 19th century. The river was

74. Bridge in 1882, looking toward Plantation. From W.J.Palmer, The Tyne and its Tributaries

forded below Byethorn and a road called Holepethe, the 'hollow road', led up to a point near the Dyvels (the old Station Hotel), following the boundary of Corbridge and Dilston townships. Thus when the burgesses decided, in 1295, to build a new bridge upstream from the ford[78], they had to reach an agreement with the Lord of Dilston which allowed them to build the southern end of a bridge on his land and to obtain a grant of way from the bridgehead to Holepethe. This way is still in use as our Station Road. In return, the burgesses paid a yearly rent of a pound of pepper and a pound of cumin.

This medieval bridge was maintained by tolls of goods passing over the bridge (there was a toll house on the north side of the bridge); rents of certain lands belonging to the bridge; and alms such as those given to the chapel of the Virgin on the bridge. This system broke down in the 16th century and the bridge became a county bridge, supported by the rates. It was very expensive to maintain and in 1661 masons reported that a new bridge, with jetties and flanker walls, was necessary. To opposition from the Justices of the Peace, who declared the proposed bridge to be 'altogether useless to our county being never otherwise serviceable than for horse and foot' the people of Newcastle presented a petition for 'one of the most ancient highways in England'.

note in the Northumberland quarter sessions order books of 1701 talks of Corbridge being 'very much dampnified' by the late floods 'so that unlesse speedy care be taken in repairing the same, the said bridge will be in danger of falling down'. It did survive the great flood of 1771, the only Tyne bridge to do so, saved by the wide floodplain on the southern approach which probably carried as much water as the river channel.[79]

a thaw, the bridge became impassable and the first man to cross on the morning of 30 December had to ride up to his saddle in water. In 1824 the water was so deep at the south end of the bridge that horses had to swim with the True Briton coach. Corbridge also experienced flooding near the station in 1883 and 1886.

In 1827 the first carriage road was built between Corbridge and Dilston and in 1832 the southern arch was opened out and the roadway was raised – previously there had been steps up to the bridge.[80]

By the late 19th century traffic had increased, and there was hardly room for two vehicles to pass, though 'it has been observed that in the coaching days the old boys on the dickey could handle their ribbons as deftly as to take a hair off a kerb stone. So we hear that they used to drive at full-tilt down the bank and could easily pass a string of lead carts without slacking their pace'.[81]

Otter Hounds at Corbridge

A new, seven-arched bridge was built in 1674 but it suffered from floods at the end of the century: a

There were more serious floods in the 19th century. In 1815, after heavy snowstorms followed by

75. (opposite).Otter hounds on bridge, c.1906

76. Wood engraving by Thomas Bewick c.1785

77. From bridge, looking north. Before 1909

78. Knott's smithy, c.1885

79. Smithy in 1927, from watercolour by Robert Bertram (1871-1953). Bertram, a distinguished artist who contributed many drawings to the County History, lived in Corbridge where in 1923 he built a house in Stanners Lane called Littlecroft, creating the gardens himself

Widening the Bridge

A decision was taken to widen the bridge by three feet, and work began in December 1880. In spite of a very harsh winter, wrote Forster, 'and no crane or scaffolding of any kind...the whole was completed without the slightest accident to man or beast. The bridge on top has a fine appearance, the old glent[82] stones being removed and instead of these a narrow curb stone runs along against the bottom of the parapet on each side'. He concluded that it was 'a remarkable specimen of design and workmanship'. A correspondent to the *Hexham Courant* disagreed: it was a 'very poor improvement...women and children are evidently not thought of as having any business in crossing the bridge or proper width would have been added to give room for a footpath'[83].

A New Bridge?

In 1928 the bridge was said to be full of potholes and the District Council declared their intention to build a new bridge. Still nothing was done and in 1934 the Parish Council complained about its very bad condition. Corbridge had to wait until the end of the war for someone to suggest traffic lights.

In 1950 the County Council wanted to lay pipes under a new footpath across the bridge, thus reducing the height of the parapet. This was then raised by a single course of stone below the coping.

On 18 February 1955, it was announced that a momentous – and drastic – decision had been taken to build a new bridge, 45' wide with a 2'6" footpath, to span the river 100 yards west and parallel to the old bridge. 'Much alteration would be necessary and a few houses, including the Willows, would disappear, along with the opening leading to the bridge, familiarly known as the Bad Bank'. In reply to a question it was said that the existing bridge could not be changed as it was a national monument. The villagers unanimously approved the scheme but it was soon forgotten.

Floods and Repair

However, the floods of 1954-5 made serious engineering work necessary in the 1960s. This entailed laying a concrete invert through the bridge, across the full width of the river, consolidating the bridge and calming the flow of water. In April 1971, despite a lot of local opposition, a new temporary bridge was erected, on the sheltered downstream side, to relieve the growing A68 traffic until the new bridge near Riding Mill, planned for the new Corbridge-Hexham bypass, was completed.[84]

Meanwhile, the temporary bridge had gradually won the affection of Corbridgeans and, in 1981, after the bypass was in operation and traffic was halved, villagers and traders petitioned against the Ministry of Transport's decision to demolish it. It went, but traffic lights and lighting were kept.

80. Temporary bridge, erected 1970, to relieve traffic.

An Archaeological Puzzle

During the work in 1960 'many old oak piles were extracted, all comparatively short and mostly round'. Thirty years later, in 1992, while North East Water was laying a new water main across the bed of the river, just upstream of the bridge, more large wooden piles were exposed as well as a substantial stone wall and a cobbled roadway. It has been suggested that the timbers could be part of the ford which pre-dated the bridge built in 1235[85].

81 and 82. Removal of temporary bridge, 1981

Main Street

At the west end of Main Street, on the north side and facing down towards the bridge, is the Angel Inn, the oldest and most

83. Angel Inn, c.1880 showing 17th century building with mullioned window

prominent pub in Corbridge. It was known as the Head Inn and its importance grew with the development of coaching in Northumberland in the later 18th century. Once a week a mail coach, running between Newcastle and

Carlisle, would deliver mail and a newspaper to the Angel which was Corbridge's posting inn until the opening of the railway.

The oldest part is the central building, still with its old window divided by stone mullions. A sundial bears the inscription EWA 1726, for Edward Winship and his wife Anne. For most of the 19th century Hall family were landlords of the Angel and the butcher George Hall's great-grand-father

was born there. His grandfather, George William (see photo on p.89) was also born in The Angel and took the lease of the Blue Bell when he married.

The east end of Main Street leads out of the village to the Newcastle Road, past Monksholme, a Jacobean building owned in the 18th century by the Gibson family though Reginald Gibson was declared bankrupt in 1786 and the property was sold. George Gibson of Stagshaw Close House bought it in 1817 and by 1827 it had become the New Inn. In the 1870s, Dixon writes, 'a man called Knott lived there, with his smithy and some cottages close to, on the Castle Way' (ie. the Newcastle Road)[86]. For many years in the 19th century there were two Knott smithies in the village, one in Main Street and the other on the bridge. Other old smith families were the Atkins in Princes Street, the Forsters in Water Row and the Coopers, first in Princes Street and later in Back Row – the last said to have been installed there to shoe the Duke's hunters.

Death of Mr John Knott

A prominent smith, he came of a noted family of blacksmiths. His father and grandfather have held the Bridge End forge before him while he had four brothers in the same occupation in the district. Of powerful physique and of huge frame, Mr Knott was a typical

The New Inn was renamed
Monksholme when it was bought
by Mr.H.S. Edwards,[88] owner of
docks in Newcastle, around 1890.
In 1891 he added a porch and the
frontage below the eaves was
restored. Cottages against the high
wall were pulled down. Then, in
1892, Edwards bought the old
brewery[89] across the road from
Monksholme (now Springfield
Mews), and converted it into
stables, with housing for his
coaches.

Early in the 19th century an old
house,[90] to the right of the
entrance to Byethorn, was pulled
down when Robert Hawthorn built
a house he called the Willows.
Remains of several ancient
buildings were discovered and it has
been suggested that there may have
been a religious house or priory
here. It was near the ancient ford
across the river, at the foot of the
drovers' road (and possibly at a
junction with the Stanegate), that
the famous Corbridge Lanx was
discovered as well as a silver cup,
now lost. The south-east corner of
the original boundary of the site of
Corbridge 'burh' is in Byethorn
grounds.

The Willows was bought in the
1870s by H.S.Edwards and
enlarged and re-named Byethorn.

representative of this ancient
fraternity of smiths...The majority of
people entering or leaving the village
had to pass the smithy....In his
younger days, Mr Knott was a
prominent member of the choir of the
church but afterwards he joined the
Primitive Methodists and for 36
years was a devoted member of that
body, holding many official positions
and devoting himself especially to the
children. He was superintendent of
the Sunday School and a well-known
local preacher.[87]

84. Charlie Knott, second
from right, and his father,
who died January 1920,
on left

In 1873 a portion of the drovers' road was granted to him 'in consideration of a new road to be made at his expense about fifty or sixty yards further to the east and leading to the same ford', and the road was diverted away from the house.[91] In 1913 Barras Reed bought Byethorn and took off the top storey, using the stone to shore up the river bank. He moved to Springfield House in 1928, selling Byethorn to Eliot Common, a Newcastle shipbuilder, but keeping the land except that portion between Byethorn and the river. The land and house were inherited by his daughter, Peggy. She was a familiar sight driving her pony and trap.

Byethorn is now the property of Sir Lawrie Barratt.

85. Byethorn, c.1910, from river

86. Entries from Bulmer's History, Topography and Directory of Northumberland, 1886, (also on p. 70)

Classification of Trades and Professions.

Academies and Schools.

Atkinson Miss Jane Eleanor, Main st.
Lowes Miss Isabella, Trinity place
Michael Mrs. Anne Isabella, Princess st.
National (mixed); Andrew Carr, master, Princess street

Agents (Special).

Nicholson John, Allan Royal Steam Co. to Canada and United States, Heron's Hill
Walker Thomas, Eley's Ammunition, Market place

Auctioneer and Valuer.

Blandford Thomas (and land agent), Dunkirk House and Post Office chambers, *Newcastle*

Baker.

Hall Miss Jane, Back row

Berlin Wool and Fancy Repositories.

McCall George, Market place
Wilson Mrs. Barbara, Market place

Blacksmiths.

Atkin Robert, Princess street
Cooper Andrew (shoeing), Market place
Knott William, Main street
Swinburne Mrs. Dorothy & Sons, Bridge End

Bookseller and Stationer.

McCall George (and circulating library), Market place

Boot and Shoe Makers.

Burn James, Princess street
Charlton Adam, Princess street
Henderson John, Watling street
Richley James, Back row
Rochester William, Main street

Brick Manufacturers.

Jameson J. & Son (manufacturers of firebricks, sanitary tubes, retorts, and all kinds of fireclay goods), Corbridge Firebrick and Sanitary Tube Works
Middlemiss John Elliott (and tile), Hill Bank Brick Works; h. Westend ter.
Walker W. & J. J., firebrick manufacturers, timber merchants, and saw mill proprietors; h. Orchard House, *Hexham.*—(See Advt.)

Builders, Stonemasons, and Contractors.

Davison Brothers (Joseph), Heron's Hill
Lawson (Michael) & Turnbull (William), Water row
Middlemiss John Elliott, Westend ter.
Robson (Michael) & Fawcett (Thomas), Back row and Market place
Surtees Joseph & Son (Ralph) (and sculptors), Orchard crescent

Butchers.

Allan Isaac, Middle street
Roddair John, Gormire row
Richley Henry, Market place
Scott Thomas, Watling street
Wade Alexander, Heron's Hill

Cattle Dealer.

Harrison James, Westend terrace

Coal Merchants.

Green John, Heron's Hill
Wilkie Robert (coal and lime agent), Railway Station

Confectioners.

Robson William, Middle street
Stobart Miss Margaret (and grocer), Watling street

Cowkeepers.

Armstrong Thomas, Ashtree Cottage
Baty Mrs. Margaret, Princess street
Fenwick Thos. & Robt., Corbridge Mill
Henderson William, Linnels Cottage
Nesbitt James (and carter), Heron's hill

Drapers.

Atkin Miss Elizabeth, Princess street
Atkin Joseph, Middle street
Atkin Robert, Heron's Hill
Daglish John, Water row
Green Mrs. Isabella, Heron's Hill
Pigg & Robson, Watling street
Richley Nicholas, junr., Water row

Farmers.

Byerley John, Farnley Gate
Bell Joseph, Linnels
Brown Thos. & Ralph, Shawwell Farm
Coulson Matthew, Shildon Lough
Cowing Chas Edward, Heron's Hill
Ellerington Joseph, Howden Dene
Forrester Thomas, Hampstead
Green John, Heron's Hill
Harle John & Sons (Thomas & Robert), Heron's hill and *Barrasford*
Hunter Thomas, Sunnyside
Johnson John N. & Thos., Linnels Wood
Lowes Michael, Farnley
Marley Miss Ann, Greenleighton
Osborn John, Prospect Hill
Reed Thomas, Town Farm
Roddam John, Shildon House
Thompson Thomas, Shildon

Fish Dealer.

Urwin Adam, Middle street

HILL STREET, CORBRIDGE.

87. William Tratham, Corbridge's first postman, in his mail cart, outside Edward Robson's shop c.1900

88. Post-office in Main Street. It moved here from Front Street in 1901

89. An example of a 'duplex' (ie double) cancellation stamp. One part cancels the stamp, the other shows the village or town number. Corbridge's number was 135.

POST OFFICE, CORBRIDGE.

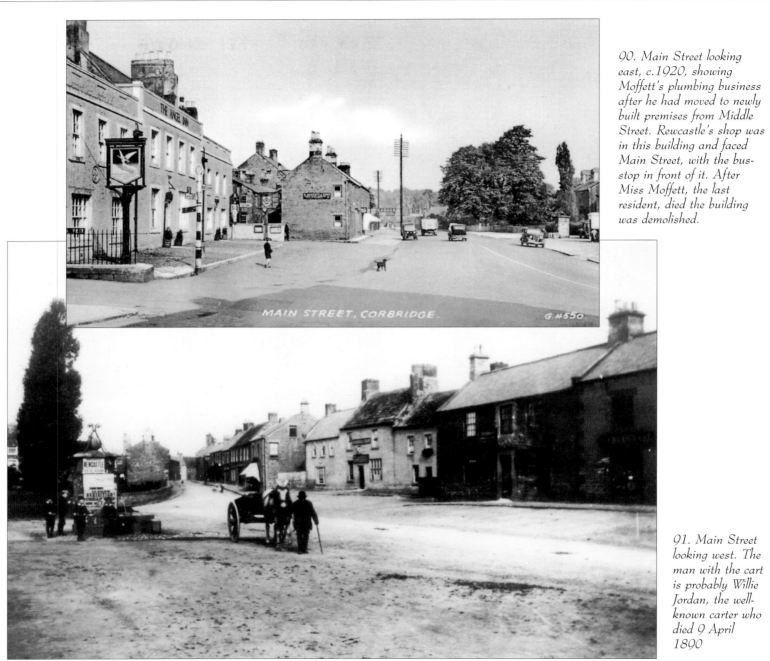

MAIN STREET, CORBRIDGE.

G.H.550.

90. Main Street looking east, c.1920, showing Moffett's plumbing business after he had moved to newly built premises from Middle Street. Rewcastle's shop was in this building and faced Main Street, with the bus-stop in front of it. After Miss Moffett, the last resident, died the building was demolished.

91. Main Street looking west. The man with the cart is probably Willie Jordan, the well-known carter who died 9 April 1890

DEATH OF A WELL-KNOWN LOCAL CHARACTER.

On Wednesday, April 9th, there died at the Union Workhouse, Hexham, a well-known Corbridge character, and who, up to the time of his removal, was the oldest inhabitant. The deceased was a native of Allendale, but had resided the most of his life at Corbridge. First he drove carts to and from Newcastle before the present railway was laid, then for some time he was a mason's labourer, but latterly he carted coals, and he might have been seen in all weathers trudging side by side along the road with his favourite "Nelly." In his younger days he was a well-known "bruiser," and many times Willie was left as sole custodian of the booths at Stagshawbank fair, and "held the bridge" against all comers. He was twice married, and out-lived both spouses. He had only one child, which died in infancy. At the Jubilee sports held in 1887, Willie figured in an old man's race. and was successful in obtaining a small prize. He was also a most valuable witness for the parishioners at the Assize trial concerning a right-of-way case. Several accounts are given concerning his age, some of which affirm he was 101 years old.

92 Death of Well-Known
Local Character: Willie Jordan

93. Main Street looking
west, before 1909

94.: Main Street,
looking west, c.1950

95. The pant, Main Street, erected by public subscription, c. 1818. Note gas lamp, removed when electric lights installed, 1962. Photo, c.1960

96. Eastfield (now Dunedin), built by Dr McLean in 1876. Photo c.1960

Gardeners (Market).

Bell Thomas, Fenwick Old Prior Manor
Bowman John, St. Helen's House
Charlton George, Heron's Hill
Donnison John, Low Riding House
Fawcett Thomas, Back row
Foggin Jos. (and parish clerk), Heron's Hill
Hall George, Middle street
Hall John, Heron's Hill
Hall Joseph & George, Heron's Hill
Martin Thomas, Middle street
Robson George (and florist, &c.), Main street
Storey William, Princess street

Greengrocer.

Forster George, Middle street

Grocers & Provision Dealers.

Akenhead George, Princess street
Bushby John, Watling street
Charlton Adam, Princess street
Davison Joseph, Heron's Hill
Fairless Joseph, Market place
Foreman George, Middle street
Greenwell Wm., Main street
Heslop Edward, Market place
Lawson Miss Ann, Water row
Marshall Richard, Market place
Stobart Miss Margaret, Watling street
Storey Adam, Watling street
Walker Mrs. Elizabeth, Princess street
Wigham Mrs. Elizabeth, Watling street

Hairdresser.

Donnelly James, Middle street

Hotels, Inns, & Taverns.

Angel, Wm. Hall, Main street
Black Bull, John Hall, Middle street
Blue Bell (New), Mrs. Margt. Gardner, Heron's Hill
Blue Bell (Old), Wm. Morpeth, Market place
Golden Lion, John Hall, Heron's Hill
Railway Hotel (and posting house), Thos. George Young, Railway Station
Wheat Sheaf (and posting house), John Summers, Watling street
Beerhouse, Mrs. E. Walker, Princess st.

'MONKSHOLME,' CORBRIDGE, FROM SKETCH MADE IN 1883.

99. Monksholme, c.1883. Sketch by Robert Bertram for History of Northumberland

100. Monksholme, 1969

101. 17th-century house, cf Monksholme, shop front by the Gas Company in the 1950s

On the north side of Main Street, next to Monksholme, is Low Hall, the oldest inhabited house in the village. Its nucleus is a 13th or early 14th-century rectangular block with ground-floor hall, with the storeyed solar at the east end raised into a three-storey tower by the Baxter family, probably in the late 15th century.[92] To the west of Low Hall is a house previously known as Eastfield (now Smiths Gore), owned by the Walker family in the 19th century. Its western half still shows a gable and mullioned windows similar to those of Monksholme, though its ground floor, which had a central four-centred doorway, was mutilated by the Gas Company in the 1950s.

Corbridge. Northumberland

Further to the west were the Old Barnes, part of a farm owned by the Walker family who also owned the Angel Inn. This was bought by Dr Hugh Maclean and in 1876 he built an imposing house on the site which he called Eastfield. It was owned earlier this century by Dr Turnbull who had his surgery there until he retired. The house was bought in 1956 by John Cecil Bishop.

The house now known as Eastfield dates from the early 19th century.

102. Drawing by Miss Edwards from S.F.Dixon, Corbridge, A Royal Saxon Town, of Low Hall showing houses against Monksholme wall

103. Low Hall, c.1900, from south

104. Premises of William Turnbull, c.1910, demolished when Bishop's garage was built in 1920. The doors led for many years to the workshop

105. Bishop's workshop, c.1930. Left to right, Stephen Bishop, Mrs Ellen Bishop, John Bishop senior and John Cecil Bishop

106. Miss Peggy Reed in front of old stables at Springfield Mews

107. Miss Peggy Reed with pony and trap on bridge

Corbridge House, on the south side of Main Street and bought by Mr Robert Waddell from the Reeds, is a handsome 18th century house and 'was the first that had slates put on the roof'. It was also the first to have a front garden, enclosed by railings from the street in spite of opposition from the Parish Council – railings which went in the last war.

The Market Place

This has always been the centre of the village, dominated by the ancient church of St Andrew where the villagers were baptised, married and (until 1872 when the present cemetery was built) buried in the churchyard. Between 1852 and 1867 there were major restorations to the church, one of the most significant being the replacement of a wooden structure at the east end, by a copy of the 13th-century lancets. The glass in these lancets was given by the six daughters and granddaughters of John and Hannah Grey of Dilston, as a memorial to Hannah, who died on 12 May 1860. One of those daughters, all of whom were married in St Andrews, became the social reformer, Josephine Butler.

The Pele Tower, on the south side of the churchyard, was built as

a fortified vicarage in the 14th century. It was a sophisticated refuge, with fireplace, cupboards, window seat, a bookrest and a vaulted basement. The property of the Duke of Northumberland, it has been used for the storage of fire brigade equipment; for the distribution of gas-masks during the last war; and in the 1970s the first floor briefly became a museum. The Tourist Information office was downstairs.

Near the church, possibly on the site of the present Methodist chapel, was the Tolbooth from where justice was administered. The Stagshaw Fair was proclaimed here, originally at the old Market Cross which was replaced in 1814 by a cast-iron one presented by the Duke of Northumberland. All sorts of entertainments from flower shows and circuses to demonstrations and, at Christmas, sword-dancing, attracted the crowds. But by the outbreak of the First World War a change was

108. Market Place in 1890s, before Jubilee Buildings erected, 1897. Mrs McCall's shop is behind the Market Cross

109. Market Place, c.1960, showing replacements for Cross. Photo c.1960

110. Original Cross from top of pant, removed to back of church. Photo, c.1960

coming. 'Corbridgean', in his column in the *Hexham Courant* in 1914, prophesied that 'We have seen the last of the shows in the Market Place. They are not wanted and they will have a hard pitch to find one anywhere now. The old spirit has degenerated, at present we are in the cinema age. The fat lady has had her day ...'

Sword Dancers

Many will remember the annual visits of the sword-dancers, the performances of whom used to evoke the greatest interest amongst the inhabitants of our village. It is many years since the last of these performances was given...The dance was chiefly executed by pitmen from the Tyne and Wear... parties of a dozen or more, each with a sword by his side and profusely decorated by parti-coloured ribbon...

It is an ingenious performance and the swords of the performers were placed in a variety of graceful positions so as to form stars, hearts, squares, circles etc and were so elaborate that they required frequent rehearsals, a quick eye, and a strict adherence to time and tune. Towards the close, each one caught

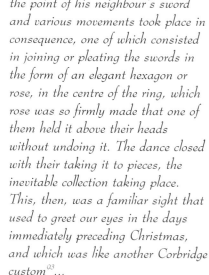

MARKET PLACE, CORBRIDGE.

the point of his neighbour's sword and various movements took place in consequence, one of which consisted in joining or pleating the swords in the form of an elegant hexagon or rose, in the centre of the ring, which rose was so firmly made that one of them held it above their heads without undoing it. The dance closed with their taking it to pieces, the inevitable collection taking place. This, then, was a familiar sight that used to greet our eyes in the days immediately preceding Christmas, and which was like another Corbridge custom[93]...

113. F.Marshall Wrothwell, chemists, Market Place.

114. Edward V11 memorial service, 1910.

Opposite page:

111. Market Place looking south, c.1911, showing Heslop's Grocery and Provision store. House built 1835. Heslops was sold in 1920 to Mr Bowler of Marshall and Bowler.

112. Market Place, c.1900.

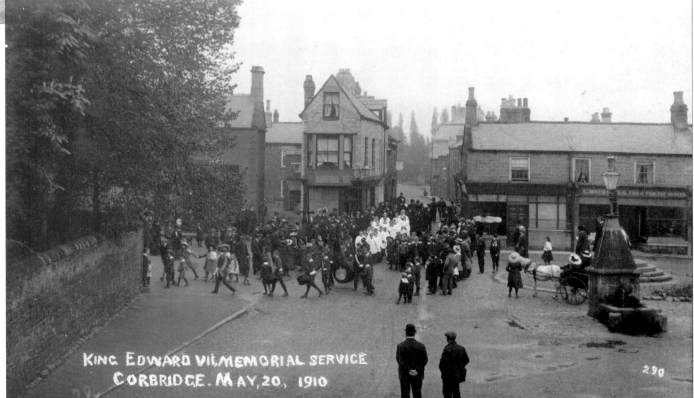

KING EDWARD VII, MEMORIAL SERVICE
CORBRIDGE. MAY, 20, 1910

Butchery and Banking

Behind the present Barclays Bank there had long been an orchard, with stables, and a house where John Richley managed his butcher's business. His brother, Henry Richley, took over the business and, in 1882, built the premises which Barclays Bank bought, 'with shop, rooms over stables, hut and land', in 1920. At that date the tenant was Donald Hall, who had been apprenticed to Henry Richley, and had rented the butchers' premises since Henry Richley's death. After Barclays bought the premises, he moved his business to Hill Street where it has remained ever since.

Mr Henry Richley, Butcher

A genealogy of from two to three hundred years belongs to this old-established concern, and during that unusually long period it has remained in the hands of the same family...now the leading butcher's in Corbridge, being patronised by the best families of the town and district. The shop is an imposing one, and occupies a fine corner position in the Market Place with a well-fitted interior. At the back is a commodious office, and a slaughter-house and cellars below; a stable and coach-house are also attached to the establishment. The slaughter-houses are a model of convenience and cleanliness, and all the cattle and sheep are put in stalls and hungered before being slaughtered for 24 hours, the carcases then being hung in the cool cellars through which is a current of pure cool air circulating. In the pork season Mr Richley makes pure pork sausages for which he is very famous for twenty or thirty miles round Corbridge[04].

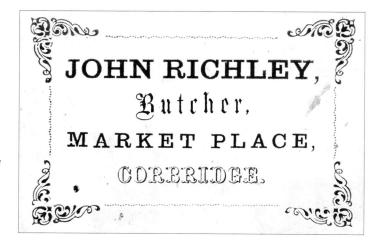

115. Trade card of John Richley (father of Henry), c.1858

116. Henry Richley, with groom, c.1870

117. Account of James
Wilson of sales for Henry
Richley at mart, March

1866, and reverse. Note high
price for tallow, used for
candles

1878

Corbridge

Geo. Fenwick Esqr
Bywell Hall

Dr to

Henry Richley
Butcher

1878

July 2	To Round Beef	32½ @ 10½	1	8 5½
17	" Leg Mutton	19 @ 10½	.	16 7½
18	" Suet	3 @ 9	.	2 3
	" Leg Mutton	12¼ @ 10½	.	10 8½
	" Steak	5½ @ 1/-	.	5 6
26	" Soup Beef	13 @ 6	.	6 6
	" Sirloin do	19 @ 10½	.	16 7½
	" Fore shine do	32 @ 10½	1	8 .
	" Half Round do	15½ @ 10½	.	13 7
	" Mutton	34¼ @ 10½	1	9 11½
	" do	36¾ @ 10½	1	12 1½
29	" Stewing Beef	32¼ @ 10½	1	8 3½
	" Leg Veal	21¼ @ 10½	.	16 7
	Forward		11.	17 1 ½

118. *Henry Richley's order for Mrs George Fenwick of Bywell Hall, 1878*

119. *Donald Hall as a young butcher in his 'Whitechapel' cart, taking delivery orders. 1915*

Martin's Bank (the Bank of Liverpool and Martin) had premises in the Town Hall Buildings since 1895, but was taken over by Barclays Bank in 1969 and closed down. In 1977, to commemorate the Queen's Silver Jubilee, the Bank gave the piece of land at the back of their building to the people of the village in order to allow public access to the river.

The first bank in the Market Place was Lambton and Co., a branch of an old bank established as Davison-Bland and Co. in Newcastle in 1788. It changed its name in 1790 and was taken over by Lloyds Bank in 1908. Lloyds closed Lambtons when they built their elegant new building on a dominating site looking down over the bridge from Middle Street in 1909. The architects were E.B. Hoare and Montague Wheeler who had a practice in Portland Street, London, between 1898 and 1937. Wheeler had done a variety of work in the north, including the Holy Trinity War Memorial church in Jesmond and the remodelling of Pallinsburn in Northumberland for the painter, Charles Mitchell, son of Lord Armstrong's partner.

When the old Blue Bell, later The Tynedale, was pulled down in 1890 the builder, Mr Davison, found an old lime-burning pit. He excavated a pit of 20 by 15 feet but judged that its original extent must have been twice this. Lime had been laid on layers of wood and so fired. The fact that wood had been used as fuel suggested a date not later than the 16th century, possible much earlier.[95]

120. Barclays Bank, 1955 (opened 1 October 1921)

121. Lambton's Bank, c.1903

122. Nicol Knitwear's Unwearoutable Socks and Shooting Socks, c.1970

Middle Street

MIDDLE STREET,
CORBRIDGE-ON-TYNE, _____ 192

ANY MAKE OF CYCLE SUPPLIED

OR BUILT TO ORDER.
LARGE STOCK OF ACCESSORIES.

Memo. from *Robt. Riddell,*

Gramophones, Records,
and Wireless Sets.

Motor & Cycle Agent

REPAIRS TO CYCLES, GRAMOPHONES, PRAMS, AND SEWING MACHINES.

MIDDLE STREET,
CORBRIDGE-ON-TYNE,

TEL. NO. 53

193

FRESH SUPPLIES DAILY.

MEMO. FROM *Robt. Riddell,*

m.

*Fish Merchant &
Poultry Dealer.*

SPECIALITIES—FISH CAKES, PORK SAUSAGE, FRESH COUNTRY EGGS, ETC.

All Orders receive our Best Attention

*123. Robert Riddell outside his cycle shop,
1 October 1913. Memo. paper from Robert
Riddell, fish and cycles*

*124 & 125 Riddell had two shops, a cycle
shop (note that you could have a cycle 'made
to order') and his fish shop next door*

*Marley Dixon had a newsagent's shop,
beside Chaffey the Baker, in Middle
Street, which he took over from the
jeweller, Bonney*

*126. Stevenson's wine shop in Middle
Street, c.1900*

127. Corbridge Carnival to raise money for charity, 1920s

128. Black Bull, photo 2000. House on the left was Usher House, owned by various members of the Usher family from 1755 to 1769

!29. Pearsons: Tailor, draper, millinery and dressmaking, c.1900.
Edward Pearson was Clerk to the Parish Council for 35 years

Front Street

(previously Water Row) leads out of the Market Place to the south-east. Here, in Mr Thomas Surtees's shop, was the village post office, run by the postmistress, Hannah Dodds, until, in April 1901, it was moved to Main Street, 'perhaps not so conveniently situated but splendidly adapted for the purpose'. On the occasion of the move, Mr Graham, the temporary 'postman in charge', was presented with a silver-mounted walking stick by the postmen, Messrs Tratham and Rutherford, and a silver matchbox by the telegraph boys. The Post Office later moved to Hill Street, where there is still a post box, and from here the last manual telephone exchange in the north was operated until 1967.

In 1886 an old thatched house in the street, one of the last in the village, was taken down. The main timbers of the roof were found to

be solid oak, held together by wood pins. Under the house, at a depth of $7^{1}/_{2}$ ft, workmen found a Roman altar, also a fragment of a Saxon Cross which was said at the time to be the only piece of Saxon work found in Corbridge.[96] The Boot and Shoe Inn was another familiar landmark in Water Row.

130. Causey House, old thatched cottage in St Helen's Street, c.1860

Watling Street

At the end of the 19th century one of the most prestigious and profitable traders in Corbridge was Edward Robson, 'tailor, drapers and men's mercer' whose premises were on the corner of Watling Street and Hill Street (after the war it became one of Jean's shops and is now a cafe). The business had been established with Mr Pigg in 1881 and Mr Robson became sole proprietor in 1887. His stock included:

worsted coatings, serges, Scotch and English tweeds, West of England and tweed trouserings, hosiery, haberdashery, men's mercery, French and English dress goods, silks, satins, velvets, velveteens, merinos, cashmeres, flannels, calicoes, sheerings, blankets, quilts, crapes, laces, frillings, ladies' silk scarves, collars and cuffs, belts, gloves, ladies' jackets, mackintoshes, ulsters, oil baizes, American leather, hollands, table covers, table cloths, shirtings, shirts, stair carpets, mattings, corsets, furs, nets, muslin, damasks, cretonnes, fancy pinafores, umbrellas, trimmings, cords, moleskins, swansdown, wools, and an infinite variety of sundries and oddments.[97]

In living memory there were many more shops in Watling Street: Larry Bamford would sell you fish and chips twice for 6d; there were two sweet shops and, beside Surtees Forster's paint shop, Tom Henderson's boot and shoe makers, and Corbridge's last saddler, Obadiah Owen. In 1939 the Hudspeths had a cafe behind their house at No 20 (now an antiques shop).[98]

131 Watling Street, looking toward Wheatsheaf Hotel, c. 1910

132. Watling Street, looking toward Wheatsheaf Hotel, showing Old Blue Bell before demolition in 1890. Note Causey House, just visible beside Wheatsheaf

*133. Surtees Forster shop,
c. 1920, with family*

EARLY 1900s

134. Hall family at door of Blue
Bell, c.1910. clockwise., Jemima,
George William, Bella, (married
Willie Maugham), Annie (married
Billy Menem) and Donald

135. The Golden Lion, c.1900

136. Woodbine House, Hill Street, c.1900

137. Bessie Smith, of Haltwhistle, outside Catharine Forster's shop, c.1920

138. Tommy Forster's haulage lorry outside Heron House with, left to right, Jack Forster, Catharine Forster, who had the shop, Billy Forster and George Davison (landlord of the Dyvels), c.1920

The Coigns

From earliest times the junction of
the road to Newcastle and the
north-south road has been a
meeting place for the village, a
kind of piazza of the north, where
people would assemble to hear the
news from travellers, or just pass
the time of day. Forster notes that
'the Coigns used to extend from
the gable of the Angel to the gable
of Mr Forster's on the opposite
side and continue at the same
width to Hill Street.'

The Narrowing of the Coigns

*The owner of the property on each
side, about a century ago (when
most people did just as they liked)
narrowed the street, dividing the spoil
between them, the owner of the Angel
Inn, for his share, getting the site of
the chemist's shop and premises; the
other the northern portion, on part of
which stands the United Methodist
Free Church.[99]*

In 1900 George Foreman had
his grocer's shop on the corner of
the Coigns, facing into Middle
Street, and it was said that 'no
better example of the best class of
shop in Corbridge could be
afforded'. In his 'handsome double-
fronted shop, with ample plate
glass windows' he stocked every

kind of grocery with a wide
selection of teas, 'skilfully blended
by experts to meet the
requirements of the
neighbourhood', Italian goods,
colonial produce, tobacco and
cigars, patent medicines,
Cambridge sausages and Wiltshire
hams and bacon. He was also
agent for Spratt's dog biscuits.

The Hirings at the Coigns

*'As every tradesman's, as well as
every labouring man's, sons and
daughters grew up…to learn to shear,
there was a general turn-out as this
was the time when higher
wages were obtained..weavers, tailors,
shoemakers, joiners,
blacksmiths..also many of their wives
and daughters. The meeting took*
*place at 7 o'clock, numbering from
100 to 150 reapers' (Forster, writing
in 1881)*

139. The Hirings , c. 1870,

The Town Hall

A 'commodious drill hall' had been built in 1875 but it blew down one wild winter night and for many years after that there was nowhere for village meetings. Sometimes the United Free Church Schoolroom on Heron's Hill was used; sometimes Mr Reed, the owner of Orchard Vale, would lend his 'long room' or granary. On 24 October 1885 the annual concert on behalf of the Reading Room and Library was held here and the Chairman, Mr Hugh Fenwick of Sandhoe, expressed his opinion that the village badly needed a large public room and that he hoped something would be done about this in the next year. Discussions started and on 6 March 1886 the well-known figure of Dr McLean, Corbridge's doctor, chaired a meeting to discuss the building of a Town Hall. It was felt that 'Corbridge had made great strides in the way of improvements during the last few years in the shape of new houses, shops, gas and footpaths, and that the proposed Town Hall would benefit the public and the shareholders'.

Mr Sisterson moved 'That it is desirable to have a Town Hall for Corbridge'. A limited company was proposed, with a capital not to exceed £2000, i.e. 1000 shares at £2 each. They wanted, besides a town hall, a reading room and library. If the villagers would take 500 shares, those on the committee would ensure that the other £1000 would be raised. Mr J.C.Straker said he would take £50, Mr Charles Straker and Mr Tully pledged support. Mr Hugh Fenwick, who could not attend the meeting, promised to take £100 or more shares should it be required.

An open competition for the design was advertised and 'a very large number of plans, some of them very elaborate' were submitted. There were so many that they had to be removed from the secretary's house to Dr Maclean's newly built house, Eastfield, in Main Street (now Dunedin), by William Jordan, the carter, who 'though 86 years of age is still hale and hearty'[100].

Frank Emley, Architect

The competition was won by a young architect, Frank Emley, who had been articled to a leading firm of north-east architects, Oliver and Leeson, then to Hodgson Fowler of Durham.

Thomas Oliver, the senior partner, of Oliver and Leeson, was the son of the architect employed by Richard Grainger to build Leazes Terrace in Newcastle. Emley would have had experience of a wide variety of designs: the firm was responsible for, amongst many other works in Newcastle, the restoration of the tower and spire of St Nicholas cathedral and the building of a block for Barclays in Collingwood Street. After qualifying, he became principal assistant to W.J.Hicks of Newcastle.

Frank Emley (1861-1938) was the fifth of a family of nine born to Thomas Emley, the head of a firm of monumental masons and ironworkers in Westgate Road. Their home was a large house in Gosforth called Ravenshill. From the age of twelve to sixteen he was at a school run by the Moravian church[101] in Switzerland which, in 1872, moved to the magnificent 16th-century Chateau de Prangins, overlooking Lac Leman. It seems to have been a broad education, with an emphasis on languages and music, games, canoeing and fishing; they even had a dark room for photography. At the time he was there 44% of the students were English and

other students came from Germany and France as well as Switzerland.

The young man worked quickly and on 18 September 1886 his finished plans were put on view. 'The entrance is by a large door in the centre, with two shops on either side. The building will be surmounted by a tower and the general appearance is very pleasing', reported a *Courant* journalist.

There were more than 30 tenders for building the Town Hall: the contract was given to the local firm, Lawson and Turnbull, and on 13 October 1886 the foundation stone was laid in Prent Street by Mrs F.M.Laing of Farnley Grange whose husband had negotiated the purchase of the land.

The Hall was 70 feet by 30 feet and could accommodate 500 people. The tower, adorned with sculptures, was the gift of F.M. Laing. In the centre of the sculpture, above a figure holding up a crown, is a copy of the famous Corbridge Seal. (The original was attached to an agreement made in 1235 by which Simon of Dyvelston allowed the burgesses of Corbridge to build one end of their bridge on his

140. Town Hall and Hill Street,c.1900

land.) It has the device 'Sigillum Commune Corbrigie' and four men's heads in profile facing one another. Other copies are outside the Angel and on the front of the Lion of Corbridge.

The first annual general meeting of the Town Hall Company was held on 5 March 1887 and the Hall was open in time for the Golden Jubilee. It immediately became the meeting place for a growing number of Corbridge clubs from cycling to the YMCA. To celebrate its opening there was a Grand Bazaar and Fancy Fair on 15 September 1887 and another on 22 October raised money for a playground for the school.

Winter 1901

Some good fairy has been transforming the Town Hall and right well it has been done... The proscenium is a work of art, columns rise on either side with ornamental capitals from which springs a semi-eliptic arch and which is the means of forming a dark background for the inner part of the stage, while the upper facades are noticeable for some

fine scroll work. Among the sides of the hall panels stand in relief with small canopies above each entrance. A pleasing effect has been given to the format of the gallery, and cornices have been run round the ceiling. The main entrance, also, has been redecorated and the hall, now, is like a bijou theatre, and one is apt to make comparisons with one of the more notable playhouses that we sometimes see.[102]

141. General view of Town Hall and Hill Street, c.1910.

142. Town Hall, c.1950, showing cinema (1943-58) and Martin's Bank (closed 1969)

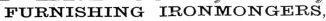
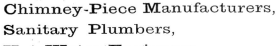

EMLEY AND SONS, LTD.,
FURNISHING IRONMONGERS,
Chimney-Piece Manufacturers,
Sanitary Plumbers,
Hot Water Engineers,
MONUMENTAL SCULPTORS,

PRINCIPAL SHOW ROOMS:
42 & 44, Westgate Road,
NEWCASTLE-ON-TYNE.

Telegrams—"Emley, Newcastle."
Telephone—Nat. 2213, 2214.

Two years after winning the competition and starting his own practice in Newcastle Emley sailed, with his new wife, for South Africa. The reason was health: he was not very strong and his family felt a more equable climate would help him. On the boat was Colonel Baden Powell who, in 1900, would command the garrison in Mafeking and become a national hero before going on to found the Boy Scout movement. The two young men became friends and Baden Powell was the Godfather of the Emleys' youngest son, Ernest Douglas.

In 1893 Emley he went into partnership with Frank Scott in Pretoria where they built the National Bank Chambers and Mint Building, which still survives. After a few years he moved to Johannesburg where, about 1898, he became partner of William Leck, a well-known architect from Belfast, in the firm of Leck & Emley. Together they produced many notable public buildings including the National Bank building—'echoed in the design of the vast new Bank City of today'. Emley designed the neo-baroque third Rand Club (1904) described by a visiting Englishman as 'barbaric, Titanic and exaggerated as the wealth of the magnates who built it'. Later, in 1920, his classical design won the competition for the central building of the University of Witwaterstrand and he was subsequently responsible for other major buildings on the site.[103]

143. Advertisement by Emley family firm in Parish Magazine, March 1909

144. Frank Emley with family in Johannesburg, c.1900

145. Sketches by Emley soon after his arrival in Pretoria

146. Staircase at Rand Club, Johannesburg, designed 1895 by Frank Emley, built 1904

147. 'The longest bar in the world' when it was built: the Rand Club

148. Architect's model for Witwaterstrand University. The University was built without the dome and the back was subsequently burnt down

The Town Hall was finally replaced as the meeting place of the village in 1922 when Mrs Edith Straker-Smith gave the present Parish Hall to the village in memory of her father, J.H.Straker.

In 1941 the Hexham Entertainment Company (owners of the Queen's Hall and the Forum) bought nine-tenths of the shares in the Town Hall Company in order to convert the building into a cinema on 'much more advanced lines than the ordinary village cinema, with Western Electric Microphonic Sound'. The cinema, which was on two floors, opened in 1943 and lasted until 1958.[104] Carr's Garage occupied most of the ground floor.

149. Emley with two of the St Bernards he bred, outside his house, Emleigh

150. St Helen's Street: Duke's Cottages, c.1960

151. Wylam and Prudhoe Cooperative, c.1900

152. Cross House, built by Eliezer Birch in 1756

Cross House and Eliezer Birch

Looking along Princes Street, past the Town Hall, one sees the imposing facade of Cross House, built around 1756 by one of the most mysterious characters in Corbridge history, Eliezer Birch. Birch is buried in the graveyard beside Corbridge church and is reputed to have given a clock to the church – but it was not the clock we see and hear today – and to have built the pant in Princes Street. Some very interesting research by R.J.Malden[105], son of R.G. Malden, Vicar of Corbridge (1947–1969), has revealed him to be a wealthy young man who, in 1745, acted on impulse as a Government spy, had a dramatic escape from the rebels; and was then forced to take early retirement due to ill health. He went first to Humshaugh, then to Corbridge which he came to love and where he acquired a lot of land. The 1779 enclosure Award for Corbridge shows his residuary legatee, Charles Potts[106] (Birch died in 1767) owning 139 acres, 1 rood and 39 perches in Corbridge' most of which he sold immediately after the Award.

Cross House is, in fact, two

houses. The stables and access to the rear were to the west; the house adjoining on the east was a pub called The Fleece Inn. In 1904 it belonged to F.M.Laing, a wine and spirit dealer. It later became a private house.

Churches and Chapels in the 19th century

When John Grey moved into his new house, Dilston Hall, in 1835, the parish church still showed signs of the destruction by the Scots many hundreds of years earlier. The chancel, chancel aisle and north transept had been only partially restored and, in the east end, the original triple lancet window had been taken out and replaced by a huge wooden one. The church had a flat ceiling and ceiling and walls were whitewashed throughout. Nevertheless it would have been quite dark because several of the windows were blocked up and there was, of course, no clerestory. This was built in 1921.

You entered the church by the door in the south wall of the chancel, down two steps as the graveyard had been raised by an accumulation of bodies in the churchyard. Well-to-do parishioners rented pews, most of

153. Pant in Princes Street, with lions' heads

154. Engraving (1823) from drawing by Rev. George Gibson, vicar 1785-1829, showing school (demolished 1830) and old window in s. transept

155 (opposite page). Watercolour of Vicarage by Lucy Gipps, 1846

which were so narrow and straight that you could not sit or kneel in them. John Grey, as Receiver and Agent for Greenwich Hospital Estates, had the grandest of all the pews: it was a large one on top of a stone structure under the first arch in the chancel, approached by a staircase from behind[107]. Beneath this were two large pews, and to the east of these sat two old men, the clerk and the sexton (they were brothers). One had a pipe to sound the keynote , the other a base fiddle. They led the singing of the psalms. No hymns were used.

In 1853 a new Vicar, Frederick Gipps (1853-74) was installed and the Dean and Chapter of Carlisle were persuaded to restore the chancel (this was part of Carlisle's ancient obligation to the church), taking away the old square pews and replacing them with pews running east and west. Those on the north side were allocated to the Receiver living at Dilston. The old musicians had presumably died or been retired, and a new organ was installed in the west end in 1844 in an organ loft supported by metal pillars and built against the tower arch which had been walled up and plastered over[108]. It was probably at this time that some fine mouldings on the capitals of the arch were broken off.[109]

The window at the east end was rebuilt, following what was presumed to be the original 13th-century form and, sometime after 1860, stained glass (designed by Wailes of Newcastle for £20) was inserted in memory of John Grey's wife, Hannah, by his children and grandchildren. The moulding underneath the east window was removed to make room for a reredos.

After Charles Grey succeeded his father as Receiver in 1864, he became one of two churchwardens at Corbridge. With the Vicar, they decided to restore the whole church, building new 'free' pews from a cargo of timber just arrived from Canada – 'a species of pine more like maple or satinwood than the pine of America or Norway... capable of a high degree of polish and new to church architecture'. The new pews allowed 500 to be seated in comfort when before only 300 could sit 'and then in great discomfort'.

A small vestry, later enlarged, was built at the outside junction of the chancel and chancel aisle and it seems likely that the north aisle was added at this time. The old pulpit and the old font were destroyed and replaced; the new font was given by the sister of the Vicar, Lucy Gipps. Many stones were found in the walls that were taken down at the restoration and some were broken, notably the memorial to William of Tynedale (removed from the church in 1929 to the Joseph Viney museum and since returned).

The ground round the chancel and on the south side of the church was lowered by two feet, and the churchyard was given paths[110].

The reopening of the church was celebrated by a general holiday, an 'exceedingly lengthy service from 11.15am to after two o'clock', and a lunch for 200 of roast beef, lobster salads and partridge pie in the large schoolroom[111]. The clerestory (J.M Martindale) was added to the church in 1921.

In 1935 Mr Reay-Smith of Riding Mill gave the altar gates (Ralph Hedley)[112] in memory of his mother and sister. The 1939-45 War Memorial was erected in the cemetery, south of the river.

In 2000, the Millennial Year, the first major 're-ordering' of the church since its 19th-century restoration is taking place. Access for the elderly and disabled is being made much easier, and there are major internal improvements, to devolop space for wider community use.

The 19th-century vicarage

When Henry Gipps was appointed Vicar in 1829 it was realized at once that he must have a new house. An architect appointed to make a survey reported that 'the dwelling house, stable and other offices are in such a state of extreme dilapidation and decay as to admit to no sufficient practicable repair but to render the rebuilding of them absolutely necessary'. The walls were built entirely of rubble stone and timber

that was not worth salvaging. There are no other records of this house but plans show a simple L-shaped building. In 1831, a new building was erected on a different site, at the north end of the Vicar's glebe.[113]

It was enlarged in 1887 when the Rev. Francis Richardson (1886-1904) arrived with three maids and seven children - clearly the house was not large or modern enough (for there were several improvements) for him[114]. When the Rev.R.G. Malden (1947-69) came, with his wife, to look at the house, he was told to 'go up the hill till you come to a place like a prison – the gates had spikes on top'. Central heating was put in at this time and the 1831 bath was found beneath the floor boards, lead-lined with taps but no outlet.

The house was sold by the Newcastle Diocesan Board in 1966 and in 1984 it was split into two houses.

Rectory lands

The two principal houses on the rectory lands were Prior Mains and the Hill Farm, and by the 17th century both were occupied by branches of the Hudspeth family. The Hill farm was sold in September 1609 to a trustee of Francis Radcliffe of Dilston and it thus passed, eventually, to Greenwich Hospital.[115]

Another branch of the family owned the Hole Farm, now Orchard Vale. This was sold by William Hudspeth to John Morpeth in 1730 and it was he who built the present house.

156. The first bath in Corbridge? Lead-lined bath, without drain, discovered under floor boards when heating was installed in Vicarage in 1960

157. Missionary Services League in Mrs Granages garden

158. Orchard Vale, built 1730. Photo 2000

159. Tennis at the Vicarage, c.1890. Rev. Francis Richardson is on right.

Dissenters

The greatest growth in congregations in the 19th century was amongst the Dissenters suggesting a real disaffection for the established church. Indeed, in the winter of 1880-1, during a severe agricultural depression, there was a complaint that the soup kitchen operating in the village was run from the Vicarage and 'in practice, the Vicar decides who might receive it'. It was said that 'coals, which are provided specially by a master of a religious communion for his own kind, may be given in heaps to those who communicate and the unwarmed poor cannot grumble, but it is a scandal when a charity raised by general subscription is administrated in an irresponsible and partial manner'.[116]

The first Wesleyan Methodist chapel was built in St Helen's Street in 1820; this was later replaced by a building in Princes Street which was restored in 1895 at a cost of £400. The seating was increased; there were more windows; the stone pillars were replaced by metal ones and there was a new 'heating apparatus'.

Primitive Methodism was founded in 1808 by Hugh Bourne, a carpenter, after he had been expelled from a Wesleyan Circuit for holding open-air meetings for the rural poor. It spread rapidly from the East Midlands 'appealing to those lower ranks of society which industrialization in both town and country appeared to have left behind'. The foundation stone for a new chapel 'on a very eligible site' opposite the Vicar's Pele was laid on 28 August 1867 when it was noted that this body of Methodists had been worshipping in Corbridge for 'upwards of 40 years but as they had no permanent place they had to conduct divine service in such places as they could secure and latterly they have had to hold their services in the open air'. The new building would cost £330: Thomas Ritson of Thornley gate was the architect and Messrs Fairless, Surtees and Walker the masons.

Opening of Primitive Methodist Chapel

The Rev R.Shields (circuit superintendent) deposited in a cavity of the stone a bottle containing a plan of the circuit, a bill of the services, a parchment with an account of the building, the names of the parties from whom the ground was purchased...with a number of coins of the realm..Mr Errington Ridley said that of many remarkable things of their time he might mention two, namely ecclesiastical edifices and female progress: 'Ladies now were not only prompt and prominent, clever and influential, but were willing and ready for every good work. Some delivered lectures and preached sermons; while others like Dr Mary Walker were proficient in surgery and medicine'.[117]

From 1849 the Wesleyans and the Reformed Wesleyans joined to create the United Methodist Free Union and they opened their first chapel in 1851. In 1885 the foundation stone was laid of a new chapel in Hill Street, on land which had been part of the Coigns, with windows copied from the old chapel at Dilston. There was a room for Sunday school that could accommodate 200 children, two vestries, one (equipped with a lavatory) for the preacher, the other 'which contains requisites for festive occasions'. The total cost was £900. In 1932 when all Methodists united in the Methodist Union, the church on Hill Street was sold and during the war the premises were partly taken over by the government.

Schools

A parish school, run by a Christopher Stocke, schoolmaster, is recorded in 1578. Under the Commonwealth, £6 out of the Bywell tithes was settled on the Corbridge School by the Commissioners for the Propagation of the Gospel. The first recorded school building was a room on the south-west side of the church, built in 1726 and kept in repair by the parish. It was demolished in 1830 and in 1835 a new vestry was erected in its place. In a trade directory of 1827 four 'academies' are listed: one of these was a high school. Another, established in 1824 in Back Row (St Helen's Street), was a 'penny' school for fifty children of the poor; there were also 'penny' schools in the other townships of the parish. Corbridge also had several Sunday schools.

But none of these was sufficient for the education of Corbridge's children, and it was apparently thanks to the efforts of the Rev. F. Gipps that the first Church of England school was built in 1855 on land belonging to Greenwich Hospital, bordered by Emms Lane (later Appletree Lane, popularly known as School Lane) with room

for 300 children.

As the population grew there was overcrowding – only 8 sq.feet was allowed per child – and by 1904 there was considerable feeling in the village that 'badly ventilated and unsanitary conditions were very materially interfering with the health of the young and rising generation'. There was no 'marching space for infants', a deficiency of playground accommodation and an absence of corridors.

The Board of Education considered that there was a need for a school for 400 children, with 10 sq.feet per child, and in 1905 Northumberland County Council Education Authority was asked to provide the increased school accomodation, with room for 150 more children, without delay. (The Education Act of 1904 had made the County responsible for schools.) The school was completely rebuilt at a cost of £1370, raised by public subscription, and opened in 1908. In 1929 a new wing was opened for additional classrooms and a museum provided for in the Will of Mr Joseph Viney, a staunch churchman. The school closed in 1970 when the new secondary school opened.

160. Primary School class, 1928

CORBRIDGE FLOWER SHOW,

Held on SATURDAY, August 29th.

When the following Prizes will be Offered :—

SCHOOL CHILDREN'S PRIZES.

127 WOMAN'S NIGHT DRESS. To be gathered into a band on each shoulder, the sleeves to be gathered into a band at the wrists. Ages of Competitors from 13 to 14.
1st Prize, 7s 6d ; 2nd, 5s ; 3rd, 2s 6d.

128 CHEMISE (For Girl about 14) To be gathered into a band round the top. Ages of Competitors from 10 to 12.
1st Prize, 7s 6d ; 2nd, 5s ; 3rd, 2s 6d.

129 CHEMISE (For Child of about 8) To be hemmed round the top. Ages of Competitors from 7 to 9.
1st Prize, 6s ; 2nd, 4s ; 3rd, 2s.

130 CALICO PATCH (3 In. Square). Ages of Competitors from 11 to 14.
1st Prize, 6s ; 2nd, 4s ; 3rd, 2s.

131 DARNING (An open Competition for All Ages up to 14).
1st Prize, 7s 6d ; 2nd, 5s ; 3rd, 2s 6d.

132 KNITTING (Man's Pair of Socks). Ages of Competitors from 10 to 12.
1st Prize, 5s ; 2nd, 3s ; 3rd, 2s.

133 PAIR OF STOCKINGS (For Child of 6 to 9. Ages of Competitors 6 to 9.
1st Prize, 5s ; 2nd, 3s ; 3rd, 2s.

134 PAIR OF MEN'S WORSTED MUFFETTES. Ages of Competitors from 4 to 6.
1st Prize, 3s ; 2nd, 2s ; 3rd, 1s.

135 MARKING IN CROSSTITCH (On Coarse Linen). The Letters A and E, and figures 3 and 9 in Scarlet Washing Thread.
1st Prize, 3s ; 2nd, 2s.

DONORS OF SCHOOL CHILDREN'S PRIZES.—Lady Aline Beaumont, Mrs Hugh Fenwick, Mrs H. T. Swan, Mrs Stephens, Mrs Greene, Mrs Straker, Mrs Edwards, Mrs C. A. P. Reed, Mrs W. Benson, Mrs Dowie, Mrs Deuchar, Miss Irving, Dr McLean.

161. Corbridge Flower Show, 1890. School children's prizes. Parish magazine, 1898

162. Two infants' classes, c.1930. Left to right (standing): Jack Robinson, Lily Robinson, Tommy Hardy, Joan Cathrae, Donald Hall, Joan Watson, Howard Cuthbert, Ethel Hughes, Geoff Sanderson, Dulcie Foster, Vera Bell, Doreen Bell, Alan Charlton, Wilfred Hopkinson, Jessie Atkin, Lowery Haugh. Left to right (kneeling) Roy Hulse, Joyce Cornish, Walter Ridley, Gladys Smith, George Cooper, Christine Kirby, Arthur Blakey Left to right (sitting) Joe Foster, Alfred

Cathrae, Andrew Tailford, Sybil Charlton, May Handiside, Margaret Hall, Richard Bell

163. School children outside Alf Charlton's sweetshop in 1920. The shop's owner, Alf Charlton, is in the doorway

In 1907 a 'Temporary County Infants School' was opened in a two-roomed building with a corrugated iron roof. Later two more classrooms were added. In 1914 there were 75 children on the register. This school lasted till 1969 having lost its 'temporary' designation in 1955 though plans for a new school had been agreed by as early as 1946.

A Corbridge County Secondary School opened in 1961 and became a County Middle School when the county organised for

164. Children at Miss Cochrane's school, Beechcroft, c. 1950
Left to right, back row:
Billy Dickinson, Anne Craig, Alison Yeeles, Colin Braithwaite, John Malden, John Baker, Jennifer Coulson, Charles Moberley, Bridget Wake, Pratt twin, Front row: Nicholas (Kiwi) Craig, Bridget Bainbridge, Derwent Gibson, David Horgan, Humphrey Reay-Smith, Pratt twin.

165. Street Parade of Corbridge C. of E. First School to raise funds, June 2000

comprehensive education.

Since the late 19th century Corbridge had had a private preparatory school, Corchester, started by the Rev. J.Scott in 1891 with one pupil in a house to the west of the village called Corchester Towers. His successor was George Smart and during his headmastership it became an excellent and thriving school, educating the sons of many of the local gentry. The boys used to occupy the pews in the north transept at Matins in St Andrews on Sunday mornings. Corchester closed in 1965.

From about 1938 to 1955 many children also attended the little pre-prep school run by Miss Cochrane at Beechcroft in the Aydon Road and known affectionately 'Cockies'.

The Railway

The Newcastle-Carlisle railway made Corbridge a commuter town and opened the way to all the building development of the later 19th and 20th centuries. At 63 miles it was the longest line so far proposed; it was also the earliest. The first idea was for a canal but finally it was decided to substitute a horse-drawn railway. At a meeting on 26 March 1825 a railway company was formed with a capital of £300,000. The Greenwich Hospital Commissioners, who owned much of the land to the south of the river, were worried, and they commissioned a survey by George Stephenson to report on the possibility of avoiding the south bank as much as possible. There was also a concern about flooding. A route was suggested along the north bank, passing the north end of Hexham bridge, but in the end the southern route was preferred.

An Act of Parliament providing that no locomotive or moving steam engine whatsoever could be used on the line was given Royal Assent on 22 May 1829. But the company soon realized that horsepower would be impractical over such a long distance and petitioned Parliament to introduce a new Bill to allow steam traffic.

Ceremonial Opening

The first part of the line was opened on 9 March 1835 by a ceremonial trip from Blaydon to Hexham 'with 600 persons accommodated in three railway carriages and several gentlemen's carriages mounted on the tracks' but all services had to be withdrawn two weeks later as Mr Bacon Grey of Styford had obtained an injunction against the use of steam traffic. There was a public outcry, Mr Bacon Grey relented and service was resumed on 6 May 1835. In October 1836 there was an early snowfall and the company tied two besoms to a locomotive to sweep snow from the rails.

The line was completed by 1838 and a grand opening was planned on 18 June, the anniversary of Waterloo. 'The day was celebrated with a ceremonial display almost unequalled in the history of railways. Many flags and banners were carried or floated conspicuously in the air'. The memory of 1815 stood out in words: 'The Glorious Eighteenth of June' and 'Vapor Vincit Omnia' – steam conquers all. After a variety of mishaps – Redheugh Quay in Newcastle collapsed and some passengers got a ducking, and the Chairman of the Company was forced to travel in an outside 'open' carriage as someone had taken his seat – the procession of trains set off for Carlisle. All but one of the Company's locomotive engines took part, with a pilot train in front carrying the Union Flag. There were thirteen separate trains holding altogether more than 3,500 passengers, and stops were made at Corbridge, Hexham and Haydon Bridge where great enthusiasm was displayed. It was a great day for rail and surely an unforgettable day for all the passengers.[118]

Yet there were frequent accidents. On one occasion several Irish cattle were run into by a train; on another the coroner reported that 'the deceased, who was a passenger alighting at the Corbridge station, did not make that effort requisite to leave the train while stationery'. A lamp exploded in the third-class carriage after a porter poured paraffin into the globes of some roof lamps 'under the curious impression that this was the proper way to supply them with oil'.

There were also complaints about accommodation. To begin with there was only first and second-class seating inside but soon 'open thirds' were provided which at first consisted of planks arranged across open goods tracks. In 1867, after the amalgamation with the Stockton and Darlington and West Hartlepool lines, there was a complaint that the upper classes were in 'cushioned carriages with hot water pans for their feet; the middle class may still pay first class fares for second-class accommodation and the working and poorer class may still be carried at inconvenient hours, in carriages made to hold 50 passengers with one light, and many draughts, at one penny farthing on some and on others one penny per mile, without any chance of getting a return fare at a fare and a half'.

166. Penalties in 1835

167. Station Road, postmarked April 1906, sent from Seal Cottage, Corbridge

But the railway proved popular and frequent special excursions were arranged, especially in the summer. In the 1840s there were special trains from Newcastle to Corbridge for the Stagshaw Bank Fair Day in May as there were a century later for the Tynedale August Bank Holiday Agricultural Show. Cheap day excursions to Carlisle on Sundays met great opposition from sabbatarians.

The line was absorbed by the North Eastern Company in 1865.

Station for Corbridge.

The first Corbridge station appears to have been built on the south of the tracks but had to be demolished because the railway company did not get permission to cross the turnpike road on the level. A bridge had to be built in 1847 to carry the road across the centre of the station spanning platform and tracks, and a new station – 'curiously like a private house with an added platform verandah and nice Tuscan columns'[119] – was built on the north side. It is now The Valley, an enterprising, and excellent, Bangladeshi restaurant.

In 1897 one could order the *Hexham Courant* at the W.H.Smith bookshop in the station and it would be delivered by their boy early on Saturday morning.

NEWCASTLE TO CARLISLE

STATIONS.	Miles	WEEK DAYS. 1	2	3	4	5	6	SUNDAYS. 7	8	9
			1 2 3 Class. a. m.	Mail. 1 2 Class. a. m.	1 2 Class. p. m.	1 2 3 Class. p. m.	1 2 Class. p. m.		1 2 3 Class. a. m.	Mail. 1 2 3 Class. p. m.
LEAVE Newcastle	......	......	6 0	10 0	1 30	4 0	6 30	......	6 0	5 0
Gateshead	......	......	......	9 50	1 20	3 50	6 20	......	......	......
Scotswood	2¾	......	6 6	10 7	1 37	4 7	6 37	......	6 7	5 7
Derwenthaugh	2¾	......	......	10 5	1 35	4 5	6 35	......	......	......
Blaydon	4	......	6 13	10 15	1 45	4 15	6 45	......	8 15	5 15
Ryton	6	......	6 20	10 22	1 52	4 23	6 52	......	8 22	5 22
Wylam	8¼	......	6 27	10 30	1 59	4 32	7 0	......	8 30	5 30
Prudhoe	10½	......	6 33	10 37	2 6	4 40	7 7	......	8 37	5 37
Stocksfield	13	......	6 40	10 45	2 12	4 47	7 14	......	8 45	5 45
Riding Mill	15½	......	6 46	10 52	2 18	4 54	7 21	......	8 52	5 52
Corbridge	17½	......	6 52	10 59	2 24	5 2	7 27	......	9 0	6 0
Hexham	20½	......	7 6	11 13	2 37	5 15	7 39	......	9 13	6 13
Fourstones	24½	......	7 14	11 23	2 45	5 25	7 49	......	9 23	6 23
Haydon Bridge	28¼	......	7 30	11 38	3 0	5 40	8 2	......	9 38	6 38
Bardon Mill	32¼	......	7 39	11 47	3 9	5 50	8 12	......	9 48	6 48
Haltwhistle	36¼	......	7 54	12 0	3 24	6 7	8 27	......	10 5	7 5
Greenhead	40¼	......	8 1	12 8	3 31	6 15	8 35	......	10 13	7 13
Rose Hill	42¼	......	8 7	12 15	3 37	6 22	8 42	......	10 20	7 20
Low Row	46	......	8 15	......	3 45	6 29	8 40	......	10 28	7 28
Milton	49	......	8 30	12 35	4 0	6 45	9 5	......	10 45	7 45
How Mill	52¾	......	8 40	......	4 10	6 55	9 15	......	10 55	7 55
Wetheral	55¾	......	8 50	12 47	4 20	7 5	9 25	......	11 5	8 5
Scotby	57½	......	8 55	......	4 25	7 10	9 30	......	11 10	8 10
ARRIVE AT Carlisle (London Road)	59¾	......	9 0	p. m. 1 0	4 30	7 15	9 35	......	11 15	8 15

Carlisle to Newcastle and Gateshead May 1849.

STATIONS.		Weekdays. 1	2	3	4	5	6	7	Sundays. 8	9	10
		1 2 3 Class a.m.	1 2 Class a.m.		1 2 Class p.m	1 2 3 Class p.m.	1 2 Class p.m.		1 2 3 Class a.m.	1 2 3 Class p.m.	
CARLISLE ....DEP.		6 0	7 45	....	12 15	4 15	5 45	....	8 20	5 0	....
Scotby		6 5	7 50	....	....	4 20	5 49	....	8 25	5 5	....
Wetheral		6 12	7 57	....	12 22	4 27	5 55	....	8 32	5 12	....
How Mill		6 20	8 5	....	....	4 35	6 3	....	8 40	5 20	....
Milton		6 34	8 18	....	12 40	4 50	6 15	....	8 55	5 35	....
Low Row		6 42	8 25	....	....	4 58	6 22	....	9 0	5 43	....
Rose Hill		6 54	8 35	....	12 55	5 10	6 32	....	9 15	5 55	....
Greenhead		6 59	8 40	....	1 0	5 15	6 37	....	9 20	6 0	....
Haltwhistle		7 8	8 49	....	1 10	5 25	6 48	....	9 30	6 10	....
Bardon Mill		7 18	8 58	....	1 20	5 35	6 58	....	9 40	6 28	....
Haydon Bridge		7 32	9 11	....	1 35	5 50	7 15	....	9 55	6 39	....
Fourstones		7 42	9 21	....	1 49	6 0	7 23	....	10 5	6 45	....
Hexham		7 56	9 35	....	2 0	6 16	7 38	....	10 10	7 0	....
Corbridge		8 6	9 45	....	2 8	6 25	7 46	....	10 30	7 10	....
Riding Mill		8 13	9 52	....	2 14	6 32	7 52	....	10 37	7 17	....
Stocksfield		8 21	10 0	....	2 20	6 40	8 0	....	10 45	7 25	....
Prudhoe		8 28	10 7	....	2 26	6 47	8 6	....	10 52	7 32	....
Wylam		8 36	10 15	....	2 33	6 55	8 13	....	11 0	7 40	....
Ryton		8 43	10 22	....	2 39	7 2	8 19	....	11 7	7 47	....
Blaydon		8 55	10 35	....	2 50	7 15	8 30	....	11 20	8 0	....
Derwenthaugh		9 0	10 40	....	2 55	7 20	8 35	....	....	....	....
Scotswood		9 0	10 40	....	2 55	7 20	8 35	....	11 25	8 5	....
Gateshead } Arrive		9 15	10 55	....	3 15	7 35	8 50	....	....	....	....
NEWCASTLE }		9 10	10 50	....	3 10	7 30	8 45	....	11 35	8 15	....
					Mail				Mail		

168. *1849 Railway Timetable.*

169. *Corbridge Station showing old signal box, c.1885. Replacement was burnt down in 1957*

On 31 July 1867 a letter appeared in the *Hexham Courant* suggesting that as the village had now become 'so celebrated for the resort of visitors' there was a great need for increased accommodation. A reply came two weeks later:

A piece of ground has been secured near the station - so close, in fact, that a gentleman may be in bed at nine and in the train for Newcastle at 9.10. An eminent architect and surveyor is at present engaged in making the plans..[120]

This Station Hotel, as it was known for many years, is now the Dyvels.

Hospitals

Corbridge secured the services of a trained nurse 'for the sick poor of Corbridge and the neighbourhood' in 1889. In June 1900 Miss Edwards of Byethorn, who had started the local district nurse fund, opened a 'District Nurses' Home and Harry S.Edwards wards' in Bank Top House which she leased from the Beaufront estate. The hospital was not intended for infectious diseases but for the treatment of 'patients of the poorer classes who cannot be adequately nursed in their own houses'. There were two wards, one for men, the other for women, each with two beds; and three bedrooms upstairs, one of which could be used as a private room. The access to the mortuary was through the doors facing the street, opposite the Wheatsheaf.

In 1913 the hospital was averaging three patients a day but the lease was due to expire in 1915 and there was clearly a need for more space. The building of a new hospital was suggested in 1914 but all plans had to be postponed until after the war.

An existing building was found and on 22 August 1918 Mr Joseph Straker, Chairman of the Cottage Hospital and District Nursing Association, conveyed to the Trustees the house and grounds of Prior House as a memorial to his wife, Mrs Charlotte Straker, endowing it with £5000. Very little structural alteration was required and the hospital opened with a three-bed ward for men, with a colour scheme of blue, and the same for women, with the addition of a cot and a colour scheme of pink. Like the earlier hospital, it was to be primarily for the use of poor people.

An increase in road traffic led to more accidents and by 1930 it was recognized that an emergency ward was necessary. This was, in part, funded by a grand carnival in Corbridge in which councillors played the parts of King, Queen and Mayor.

In May 1947 it was acknowledged that the Charlotte Straker hospital was meeting a definite need, having treated 346 patients in the last year. Until the 1960s it had an operating theatre where GP anaesthetists would work with consultants from Hexham hospital. But gradually it became more of a geriatric

PROPOSED SCHEME FOR SECURING THE SERVICES OF A TRAINED NURSE.

"A suggestion having been made that the services of a trained nurse would prove a great boon in many ways to the sick poor of Corbridge and the neighbourhood, it has been taken up by several of the residents in the vicinity. A meeting was held at the Vicarage on December 19th, 1888, at which the Vicar presided, when it was resolved to form a committee of ladies to carry out the scheme. This committee has been formed, and the members of it being fully persuaded of the benefit and comfort that would be experienced by the sick poor from the services of such a nurse in their own homes, venture to appeal for subscriptions to enable them to bring this about.

It is estimated that the sum of from £60 to £70 per annum will be required to meet the nurse's salary, and several other incidental, but, at the same time, indispensable expenses. Subscriptions and donations for this purpose will be gladly received by the hon. secretary, or by any of the members of the Committee. Any gifts of old linen, sheets, blankets, various nursing appliances, beef tea, &c., will also be very acceptable.

The members of the committee are :—

MRS. EDWARDS.	MRS. C. A. P. REED.
MRS. GREENE.	MISS RICHARDSON.
MISS HARRISON.	MISS STRAKER.

MISS E. M. EDWARDS, Hon. Sec."

The above speaks for itself. It is only necessary to add here that the services of the nurse will be free to the poor ; while those who can afford it may secure the same by the payment of a small fee.

"I was sick and ye visited me." With these words ever before us nothing further need be urged in favour of the scheme to Christian friends ; if, after due consideration, it appears that in this way the conduct thus highly honoured may be imitated, liberal support will doubtless be given.

Is it not thus that we may " bear one another's burdens, and so fulfil the law of Christ "?

170. Proposed scheme for securing services of a trained nurse, Parish Magazine, December 1889

171. Raising money for cancer research 1990s

NHA has voted to close Corbridge Hospital

Hospital closure protest grows

'CHARLOTTE' GOES BACK TO CORBRIDGE – FOR NOTHING!

Headlines in Hexham Courant, 14 February 1986, 4 April 1986, 15 December 1989

hospital, at a time when care of the elderly was still part of the NHS. From about 1975 its future was in doubt and in October 1988 the Northumbrian Health Authority announced its closure in order to provide money for a new hospital for Wansbeck.[121]

Thanks to a tremendous village effort, coordinated by Dr Graham Grant and the committees of the Charlotte Straker Project Trust, the NHA agreed in 1989 to make the property and land over for development by a housing trust and £300,000 was raised by the Trust in 18 months. It re-opened in 1992 with a new wing, bed-sitting rooms and flats. Eight sheltered housing bungalows were

built, and the whole hospital was refurbished with extra care accommodation, new furnishings and medical equipment.

Maternity Home

In August 1930 it was announced that the Nursing Home of the Tynedale Benefit Nursing Association was to move from Ovingham to Ealesfield House on the south side of the bridge in Corbridge. Miss Williamson, secretary of the Association, masterminded the project. It soon became a maternity home, the only one between Newcastle and Carlisle, and did not close until 1969 when the Maternity wing in Hexham hospital was opened. The building was bought and became a hotel, The Lion of Corbridge, which opened in 1973.

The Red Cross

In 1911 Dr Noel Jackson had opened a women's detachment of the Red Cross in his home, Riverhill, and members worked as VADs[122] in the Dilston hospital during the 1914-18 war. A men's detachment started in 1927, with the first ambulance. By the end of 1939 there were three ambulances, a First-Aid post and an 'excellent personnel' serving the district from Bellingham to Wylam. In 1951 they obtained their own hall, in St Helen's Street.

Luck, Ill-Luck and Cures

Before the development of scientific medicine, superstition played a large part in most people's lives:

It was unlucky to be sole owner of a hive of bees, or to kill a spider...Cock-crowing at the door was an intimation of a coming visitor...Blacksmiths will never light their fires on Good Friday. Three raps are heard before a death. Salt is often put upon a cow's back immediately after it has had a calf. It is also put upon a child's tooth when it comes out and the tooth is then thrown into the fire while some doggerel is spoken over it. There are some odd customs about bread, such as never turning a loaf upside down, or a ship will soon be in that position. If a nail prick a man or beast, it must be put into the fire; and to heal a sore throat the left-leg stocking must be tied round the neck. A child's nails must always be bitten off, or else it will become a thief...[123]

Whooping cough: Carry children through the smoke of a lime kiln or put a trout's head into the hand of a child affected.

Ringworm: Go to a charmer before sunrise where the place affected is rubbed with earth beneath a gooseberry bush.

It is counted lucky to carry in the pocket a crooked sixpence, or one with a hole in it, or to put a stocking on through inadvertence inside out. People with meeting eyebrows are thought fortunate fellows. It is lucky to set a hen on an odd number of eggs; set her on even ones, and you will have no chickens. Again, if two persons wash their hands together in the same basin they will fall out before bed-time[124]

Cure for cattle plague

You should give to all your Cattell, as well the sound as the sicke, this medicine, which never failed to preserve as many as have taken it. Take of old strong urine a quart, and mix it with more than a handful of hens dung well dissolved therein and give it to your beast to drink.[125]

172. Charlotte Straker Hospital today from bungalows. New wing with flats on left

Museums

Over the years, there have been collectors who have shown their objects to the public. In 1828 Bartholomew Lumbly, 'a man of some means and eccentric in his character... built on his own property in the Market Place and on the west side of his dwelling house...a very neat and tastefully designed square building with a battlement on all sides, which he appropriated to the exhibition of a collection of curious and interesting articles, such as are common to museums; a small garden was attached to it, extending down to the river, which was laid out with great taste and beauty and was at the time, one of the 'lions' of Corbridge'. At his death his Will was disputed and when the rightful heir was at last named he got rid of the 'objects' which were 'carted down to the riverside where they were destroyed'[126].

The earliest known Corbridge collector was the Rev. John Walton, Vicar from 1742 to 1765 and friend of the great antiquary, William Stukeley. By his Will he bequeathed 'my altars, fossils and cabinets, with medals, coins and intaglios and my pictures to the archdeacon of Newcastle, provided he is willing to pay £60, £50 or £40 for them'[127]. His collection of Roman and other antiquities was sold by his executors and seemed to have vanished. However, it is at least possible that one of these Roman pieces found its way to Corbridge's first real village museum[128].

In 1929 the Viney Museum was opened in a new wing of the C.of E. school by Mrs J.C. Straker, supported with money from Mr Joseph Viney who had done many things in his long life, including property development. Some thirty years earlier, he had built a row of houses at the bottom of Aydon Road, one of which, Highclear, he kept for himself and in which he died at the age of ninety-nine.

The *Hexham Courant* of 11 January 1930 reported that

Many of the Roman remains from the collection of the late Mr John Clayton have found, through the generosity and instrumentality of Mrs J.C.Straker of Stagshaw House, who displays a keen interest in things of this nature, their way to a permanent place in the Joseph Viney Museum, attached to the Corbridge C.of E. school[129].

'If any place upon Tyneside deserves a museum it is

173. Portrait of Joseph Viney on horse

Corbridge,' said the Vicar, Mr Blackburn. It contained, amongst other things, 'a huge oil painting of the donor; Roman altars, some from St Andrews' Church, others from Chesters and other Roman sites; bronze vessels from Corstopitum; Roman bodkins and needles; a fine collection of fossils lent by the Hancock Museum; a piece from the S.S.Forfarshire (Grace Darling's ship); a piece from Derwentwater's coffin'; and

'as fine a collection of seahorses as any in the North of England'[130].

In the 1950s, when the school-leaving age was raised, the Museum became a classroom. The old school buildings were sold in 1970, the bulk of the collection having disappeared by then or been returned to the lenders. Viney's name is perpetuated in Viney Cottage, the house converted from the old museum, and in two brass plaques in St Andrews, commemorating him and his second wife, Annie.

Obituary of Joseph Viney, died 12 February 1928

Joseph Viney was born at Easingwold and lived in Corbridge 54 years. From the age of 11 he travelled the Yorkshire markets with his auctioneer father, visiting Northallerton, Leyburn, Richmond and York. Stalls could be loaned from the market keeper on payment of 6d and without asking his father's consent he decided to hire one of the stalls and commence a bazaar. The bazaar business proved too quiet for his energetic disposition and he decided to commence a circus of broken-in ponies etc when only 14 years of age. At the age of 21 his father died and he was left to carry on his father's business. Moving to North Shields, they were at first unable to procure business premises but becoming acquainted with a sawyer he obtained an old ship's mast and by cutting it into deals he was able to build a shop on the New Quay at North Shields...He was an ardent churchman and a staunch conservative. He was married three times...[131]

174. Princes Street, 1910, showing houses built by Joseph Viney in Aydon Road, c.1890. One of these is Highclear in which he died

Roman Site Museum: English Heritage

A new museum, single-storied with an exhibition area of 200 square metres, opened at the Roman site in 1983. It was designed by the Napper Collerton Partnership who made much use of natural materials - sandstone, timber and blue slate. The exhibition, which is in the central area, faces the Roman remains. To reach the site - an easy walk from the village - you go through the exhibition area in which panels trace the history of the Roman occupation with the aid of many sculptures and other objects found on the site. In 1999 the Corbridge Lanx was on loan from the British Museum for a period.

The First Parish Council

The Local Government Act of 1894 provided for parish councils to be set up to take the place of a variety of local government (mostly church) councils. There were approximately 800 amendments to the Act and for some months after it came into force the *Hexham Courant* found it necessary to print a weekly column by a barrister to help the public to interpret the Act.

The Corbridge Parish Council held its first meeting in January 1895[132] and Mr Jameson, the owner of the potteries, was elected chairman. It, too, was not sure of its powers and when a member of the Council suggested that they go through the books of the Vestry Council, the Clerk decided that there was not anything there that they were entitled to. They ordered themselves a bag for books and a safe and arranged accommodation for themselves in the new Town Hall for £12 a year.

Oddly enough, one of the Council's first decisions was to change the names of Water Row to Front Street, Heron's Hill and Scramblegate to Hill Street and Back Row to St Helen's Street. Since they had also voted to exclude the public there appears to have been no public discussion, but the decision was to be challenged several times, notably by the historian Percy Hedley and, in 1947, by Professor Daysh of King's College who 'had encouraged his colleagues in Town and Country Planning to carry out certain investigations in Corbridge and thought the reintroduction of street names might help considerably in the proper appreciation of the character and

function of Corbridge'. On both occasions, the Council decided that though the old names sounded better, a change would be too much trouble.

Another early concern was Corbridge's charities. Many of these dated back several hundred years and related to the ecclesiastical parish constituting, in addition to Corbridge village, Aydon, Aydon Castle, Clarewood, Dilston, Halton Castle, Thornbrough, Great Whittington and Little Whittington. As the new Parish Council was concerned only with the village of Corbridge, they could not, unlike the old Vestry Council, be responsible for the charities. A board of trustees had to be appointed.

The main concerns of the Council, then as later, seem to have been water, lighting and footpaths.

For many years the village relied on water brought from springs. There were pumps in Main Street, the Market Place and by the Wheatsheaf Inn, and springs running into troughs below Monksholme in Spoutwell Lane, at the foot of Priory Gardens, Princes Street at the foot of Appletree Lane and St Andrews Well at the foot of Wellbank on

the old Carlisle Road (Carelgate) to the west of the church. But in the 19th century demand for water rose and standards of hygiene rose too. In 1818 the Duke presented a pant to the village in the Market Place; another was erected in Main Street by public subscription.

Later in the century Corbridge grew concerned for its reputation as a health resort. Water in the Market Place became discoloured in wet weather and ran short in dry weather. The Princes Street pant had two spouts: one was contaminated by drainage and the other was found to contain carbolic acid and petroleum poured from a neighbouring yard. A correspondent to the *Hexham Courant* complained of 'much vegetable matter and great numbers of animal dead and decaying, the species of which I know not'. In 1882 the water supply was reported to the local sanitary committee as defective. As a result, a new Water Scheme was planned, and completed in 1887,

the supply being obtained from the celebrated Shaw Well Springs on the Stagshaw Estate. The residents of Corbridge owe a debt of gratitude to the late John Straker, Esq., for the very generous terms upon which he granted the supply. During the long drought of the past season, it was generally remarked that the great influx of visitors to the town, was attributed in a great measure to the ample water supply, which was found sufficient not only for domestic but for all other requirements of the place.[133]

Yet contamination continued and led to disease. In 1915 there was a serious outbreak of diptheria though Corbridge avoided Newcastle's cholera epidemics. Private individuals diverted water for their new 'flushing tanks' which in one case at least communicated directly with the village water supply. There were complaints about rubbish: the disgrace of public lanes. In 1905 'Corbridge was a little worse than the other villages of its kind in respect of the tippage of rubbish'. While at one time gardeners would cart away the middens for what they were worth, 'with the increase of tinned goods, the ashpit became the receptacle of lots of things that are taboo to gardeners'.

There were 'abominable' smells on the bridge and a need for a

175. Letter from Corbridge Gas Company, confirming times of lighting. Note no lighting at full moon

public urinal. But even this public-health move was contentious, one councillor complaining that there were 'plenty of secluded places in the village'. A correspondent to the *Courant* sighed that 'this is the sanitary age. If you cannot find a smell, the authorities will do it for you'[134]

In 1920 it was reported that the supply to the north side of the village, from Holley Hole Farm and Shaw Well was 'pure, wholesome and plentiful in quantity and has no action on lead piping'. On the other hand, the supply to the south side was very soft and reacted with the lead and iron utensils to create carbonic (?) acid. Here the lead pipes were replaced by tin-lined pipes.

The water problems of the village were not finally solved until the Water and Sewerage Act of 1944 when water was transferred to the general rate and £60,000 was spent on a new water supply for Corbridge.

Lights Off

Lighting was even more contentious. The power to implement the Lighting and Watching Act of 1833 was transferred in 1895 to the Parish

Council. But lighting had been paid for by private subscription and now that there was a Council few people were prepared to subscribe. The Chairman called a parish meeting[135] to agree a lighting rate: lighting, he said, could not now be carried by subscription and it was for the ratepayers to say yes or no. 'If they say 'no' then the place will go in darkness'.

Mr Joseph Fairless proposed that the township 'be not lighted by the rates' and his motion was won by 30 to 26. The Chairman pointed out that any ratepayer could demand a village poll to reverse the decision, at which a voice from the back shouted 'We will double-lick you if it comes to a poll'.

So the village remained in darkness for the winter of 1895-6 and then the decision was reversed and the lights went on again, 'except for seven days each month nearest the full moon'. And, as one Councillor said, 'the nights when it was supposed to be full moon were often the darkest they had'.

Gas, Electricity or the Moon

It was not until 1929 that all-night lighting was agreed at the south end of the bridge, the Coigns, Cross House, the top end of Watling Street, Monksholme and the Market Place. But this was still gas: Corbridge streets were not lit by electricity until 1962. By that time the church and the cottage hospital had had electric light for more than thirty years. And it was sixty-five years since a Corbridge correspondent, writing of the Corbridge Electric Lighting Company, described the many advantages of electricity over gas.

Electric lighting is now so general in town and small country districts that it need not surprise the general public to find Corbridge going in for this modern means of illumination...(It gives) a steady light; does not substract oxygen from the air; people are healthier in electric than gas works; it does not smoke ceilings, damage books or tarnish silver; it is more easily controlled by switches; there is no damage and no objectionable smell; it costs the same or less; there is no danger of explosion; it can be used for the decoration of shops in a way impossible for gas[136]

We don't need an almanac to tell us when the moon should be shining.

Any night after 6pm if the streets are not lighted you can bet your last dollar there is a moon knocking about somewhere although its placid countenance may not be exposed to you poor mortals.[137]

Another contentious issue was the new electricity poles: the village hated them. It was suggested that they be painted but the Electric Company said that it was impossible to paint over creosote, even with 'alluminated' paint, but that they would try to decorate them with finials. The telegraph poles also came in for criticism:

Small wonder that some of the inhabitants are up in arms. These poles may be essential to the conduction of messages but they are anything but pretty, our rural scenery, the quaintness of our streets, the beauties of our kitchen gardens and the secrecy of our backyards are in process of extirpation...The poles may be essential but we might have had them a little more ornamental, and since they are such an unwholesome necessity, they might be utilized to hike the clothes lines to, in fact there are many uses they might be put to[138]*...*

Trades and Manufactories

Corbridge has, in its history, been famous for its iron-working, its shoes, its spinning and its gardens. On the first Ordnance Survey map of 1862 there is a 'Spinning Bank' running down to the bridge. This map also shows the large quarry to the north of Piper Close, now cut through by the motorway. Stone from this quarry was taken to build Newcastle's High Level bridge in 1847 because it was hard and durable.

In the 1840s there were two potteries for making firebricks, retorts and sanitary pipes to the north of the village, owned by two big landlords in Corbridge, the Walker and the Richley families. There was also a public saw-mill near the station. Walker's Pottery closed in the 1890s. The land was owned by the Straker family whose company, the Milkwell Clay Company, continued to quarry the clay until 1967.

In the last war some of Walker's kilns in Milkwell Lane were used for storing newsprint for the *Newcastle Journal* and they continued in use until 1965.

*176. Pottery workers at J.Jameson &
Sons Fireclay Works, Corbridge, 29
August 1904*

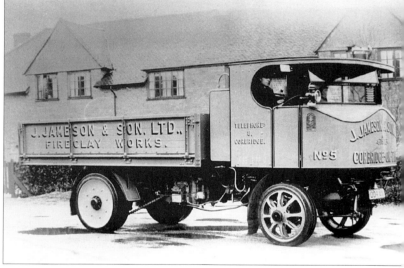

177. Steam wagon, built by Mann of Leeds and used by J. Jameson & Sons

178. Jameson lorry delivering goods

179. Circular kiln, Jameson's Pottery

180. Jameson's Pottery. Two bottle kilns, 30ft diameter.

181. Demolition of pottery chimney

182. High-Level Quarry, 1860s

AA *Archaeologia Aeliana* (Society of Antiquaries of Newcastle upon Tyne)
Procs. Soc. Ants. *Proceedings of the Society of Antiquaries of Newcastle upon Tyne*
HC *Hexham Courant*

[1] H.H.E.Craster, *History of Northumberland*, vol.x,1914, 2

[2] Discovered during the building of the A69 Hexham and Corbridge bypass in 1974

[3] Via Howden Dene, where Selkirk has detected a legionary-sized temporary camp, and a paved ford in Clocky Burn, on Peepy Farm, where a Roman brooch and coins were found. He has also followed the road west on the line described by Hodgson in *History of Northumberland*, vol. iv. See Selkirk, *On the Trail of the Legions*, 1995, 111ff.

[4] George Jobey, 'Palisaded Enclosure: A Roman Temporary Camp and Roman Gravel Quarries', AA 5th series, vol.vii, 1979

[5] 'The Roman cemetery appears to have been on the west side of the Cor Burn for immense quantities of bones have been discovered from time to time, and when, a few years ago, the course of the burn was altered, apparently to its original channel, and the cliff sloped, whole skeletons were unearthed, beside several Roman venel stones'. W.W. Tomlinson, *Comprehensive Guide to Northumberland*, 1889, 10th ed.1923,

137. Subsequent excavations have confirmed this and found other sites.

[6] English Heritage, *Corbridge Roman Site Guide*, 1989. See also John Gillam, 'The Roman Forts at Corbridge', AA 5th series, vol.v, 1977

[7] There were still two mills in the late 18th century. Annotations (1763 and 1797-8) to a 1736 Greenwich Hospital survey map show a High Mill on High Mill Acre, owned by the Duke, and, closer to the river, on 'Miller's Land', Corbridge Low Mill, on the site of the present mill. PRO MPI/230. See also Craster, op.cit.,133 and 136-7

[8] An archaeological excavation in 1993-4 revealed a series of medieval walls, representing a complex of stone buildings aligned east-west which are thought to be the remains of the manor house and church. Ryder, *Archaeology in Northumberland*, 1993-4, 27

[9] Information in this section is from M.C.Bishop, *Corstopitum: An Edwardian Excavation*, 1994

[10] Rosemary Cramp, 'Bernicia before Wilfrid' in Tom Corfe (ed.), *Before Wilfrid*, 57

[11] I am grateful to Dr John Blair, for this information. See also John Blair, 'Anglo-Saxon minsters: a topographical review' in John Blair and Richard Sharpe (eds) *Pastoral Care before the Parish*, *227ff*, especially the section on curvilinear enclosures.

Dr Blair is now working on his forthcoming book, *The Church in Anglo-Saxon Society*

[12] N.Pevsner, *Northumberland* (Buildings of Britain),1992, 236. See also G.W.D.Briggs, 'Sculptured Anglian Masonry in the Tower at Corbridge', AA, 4th series, vol.xxxix, 1961, 363-6

[13] The interpretation of the finds by Tyne and Wear archaeologists is disputed by Raymond Selkirk who believes the structure is a Roman jetty

[14] Peter Ryder, letter to author 29.7.2000

[15] Craster, op.cit., 56

[16] On 28 February 1927 the Parish Council minuted, in reply to a letter from the Home Office, that 'they had no objection to the fair being abolished'. NRO PC 57/4

[17] R.Forster, *A History of Corbridge and its Antiquities...*, 1881,65-8

[18] K.J.Bonser, *The Drovers...* 1970, 134, quoting from *A General View of Agriculture in Northumberland*, 1797, by John Bailey (1750-1819) and George Culley (1735-1813)

[19] John Hodgson in 1830

[20] M.Ellerington, *A Brief History and Guide of Corbridge*, c.1886, 33. Ellerington was a nephew of Robert Forster, above, and this is a shorter version of his uncle's work, with advertisements. He had a watchmaker's business in Water Row

(Front Street)

[21] Craster, op.cit., 98, quoting from a survey of Lord Percy's property in 1352 and the survey of property in Corbridge belonging to Hexham Priory, made in 1379 and known as the Black Book

[22] A lineal descendant was the butcher, Henry Richley, Forster, op.cit 101.

[23] 'The uprights being all in front of the horizontals, riveted and clasped alternately and the spaces between the perpendicular bars being filled with oak planks', cf. contemporary door at Bywell Castle.'A mode of construction different from the Scottish'. C.J.Bates, *The Border Holds of Northumberland*, 1896, vol.i, 377

[24] W.S.Gibson, *Historical Memoir of Northumberland...1862*, 95

[25] Gibson, op.cit., 97

[26] Quoted in Craster, op.cit.,141

[27] When a copy of the Award was presented to the Society of Antiquaries in Newcastle, R.O.Heslop 'showed the division of the Town Lands into East, West, North and Little Fields and the sub-division of these again into 1032 tillage strips, covering an area of 1225 acres. Strips were held by 45 freeholders, whose holdings lay scattered through the various fields...' . Mr F.W.Dendy 'explained the detail shown on the map and pointed out how clearly they showed the usual characteristics of the common field system. All the houses

appeared clustered together in the village and there was an entire absence of either habitations or other buildings on the land which lay outside the village. The land was divided into the usual three large fields and in this case there was also a smaller supplemental fourth field which was not very uncommon'. Procs Soc.Ants, vol,vi, 161

[28] HC 12.7.1879

[29] Forster, op. cit.,116

[30] Josephine Butler, *Memoir of John Grey,* 1869, 156

[31] Pigot's Trade Directory, 1834

[32] Butler, op.cit.,159

[33] Ellerington, op.cit., 53

[34] John Hodgson, 6.5.1830, reported in Forster, 71

[35] Forster, op.cit.,93

[36] They were said to have been fed on salmon because so many were caught in the river

[37] Forster, op.cit.,75-7

[38] 'Dying crafts of the North', HC 27.4.1935. There were many cloggers in Corbridge in the 19th century

[39] Craster, op.cit., 209, quoting parish register

[40] HC, winter 1867. This year saw one of many serious outbreaks of the acute, highly infectious virus disease known as murrain, cattle plague or, later, rinderpest. No cure was known and in the 18th century 200 million cattle died of it in Europe. The risk of infection increased with the growth in population and import of cattle in the later 19th century and the disease was devastating to agricultural communities. See Bonser, op.cit.,93ff

[41] HC 29.1.1881.   .

[42] This was the election following Gladstone's so-called Midlothian Campaign in which, in a series of speeches, he attempted to create a popular front of moral outrage against the imperialistic exploits of the Conservatives

[43] HC 3.4.1880

[44] In 1881 there were complaints about the annual boating regatta, 'a scene of shouting, swearing and bad company as can only be seen at a race meeting...many (of the visitors) are low hulking fellows of the dog-fancying and pigeon-flying class'. HC 26.3.1881

[45] 'When their backs were above water the signal was given, two or three guns being in readiness. If near enough they were usually killed and brought to land by a terrier. .' Forster, op.cit.,14 fn .

[46] Ellerington, op.cit.,68

[47] Forster, op.cit.,71

[48] 'The saddest sound that can be conceived is when the lame old bells try to break into a merry peal'. HC 12.2.1881

[49] On 9 December 1944 a memorial tablet to Robert Rowland Richley (1869-1942), was placed in the church. He had been a chorister, bellringer and churchwarden for 60 years, and one of the earliest members of the Guild

[50] HC 18.6.1887

[51] published HC 26.9.1901

[52] In the church accounts of 30 July 1767 there is an item 'To balance and starting up clock in Corbridge', £13.14s 7d. NRO EP57/27. For many years a Mr Ridley was paid £1 a year 'for winding up and cleaning church clock'

[53] HC 26.6.1897

[54] From a poem in Corbridgean's column, HC 5.1.1901

[55] HC 26.9.1900

[56] HC 25.5.1901

[57] HC 17.11.1901. George Hall remembers being shown a letter from T.C.Forster in which his grandfather, George William Hall, was mentioned

[58] This was probably Mrs Ann Allcroft, who, in 1881, was 70 years old and lived in Back Row (1881 census). She described herself as a field worker

[59] HC 12. 9.1914

[60] HC 12.9.1914

[61] HC 22. 5.1915

[62] HC 11.11.1939

[63] HC 23.12.1939

[64] HC 16.9.1939

[65] A very successful mutual insurance company whose first Corbridge lodge, in 1867, was at the Black Bull in Middle Street HC 14.2.1942

[66] HC 20.9.1939

[67] HC 20.9.1939

[68] Regulation issued by the Ministry for Home Security, reported in HC 16.9.1939

[69] Announced by the Home Secretary, Mr Emanuel Shinwell, 7.2.1947. *Annual Register,* 1947

[70] HC 24.3.1972

[71] HC 23.4.1950

[72] HC 14.8.1950

[73] Mrs Merkin, who still lives in the village, remembers doing the window with red, white and blue flowers

[74] HC 5.6.1953

[75] HC 14.1.1955

[76] Successor to the much-respected and liked J.C.Proctor

[77] Walter R.Iley, *Corbridge, Border Village,* 1975, 208

[78] In the late 19th century traces of the 1235 bridge could still be seen at low water. These consisted of the oak tie-beams by which the pier foundations were braced together. 'An accumulation of gravel has covered the line of facing-stones, and the portion

of a cutwater of the older bridge, which were visible two years ago in the bed of the river beneath the northernmost arch of the present bridge'. Tomlinson, op.cit.., 141.

[79] Information on floods from David Archer, *Land of Singing Waters* ,1992, 92ff.

[80] Evidence given in dispute about right-of-way through the Plantation, reported HC 12.7.1879

[81] HC 11.12.1880

[82] Middle English, shiny or slippy, OED

[83] HC 20.4.1881

[84] Robert Robson, *Bob's Bridges, 1998* 128

[85] Robin Sermon, *Archaeology in Northumberland*, 1992-3.

[86] S.F. Dixon, *History of the Saxon Royal Town of Corbridge-on-Tyne*, 62

[87] HC 24.1.1920

[88] In the 1881 census he described himself as Proprietor, Graving Dock, employing 300/500 men

[89] 'A malting and malt bin, with a dwelling house and outhouses and gardens adjoining having lately undergone a thorough repair..and situated in the village of Corbridge in fine barley country' were advertised in the *Newcastle Courant*, 2.10.1813. The brewery, which had been in operation since the 18th century, probably closed when the New Inn

became a private house. See also Dixon, op.cit.,58

[90] This was a 17th-century house, belonging to a branch of the Carnaby family. Craster, op.cit.,173

[91] Forster, op.cit., 99

[92] Pevsner, op.cit., 238

[93] HC 15.12.1900, drawing on a description in the *Newcastle Courant* of 26.12.1879

[94] *Descriptive Account of Hexham and Corbridge...c.1895*

[95] R.O.Heslop, 'Note on an Old Lime Burning Place found at Corbridge'. Procs, Soc.Ants NS vol.iv, 1891, 254

[96] HC 2.4.1886

[97] *Descriptive Account*. etc

[98] Information from Mrs D. Young

[99] Forster, op.cit.,57

[100] HC 10.4.1886 Jordan was baptised in Allendale in May 1800

[101] The church was founded in 1457 by the followers of the martyred John Hus who had wanted to return the church to the simplicity of the early Christians, living in a community and using the language of the people. Frank Emley's wife, Annie Fletcher, came from Yorkshire, and may have known the Moravian community at Fulneck, an important Moravian settlement near Leeds. It is interesting that some fifty years earlier, John Grey's wife, Hannah, went to the

girls' Moravian school at Fulneck. See A.R.C.Bolton, *The Six Brides of Dilston*, 1984, 28.

[102] HC 19.10.1901

[103] Information about Frank Emley from Corine Emley, his granddaughter. For early buildings in South Africa see D.P.Seymour, *Historic Buildings in South Africa*, 1989 and R.de Villiers, S.Brooke-Norris, *The Story of the Rand Club*, 1976, and article by Professor Dennis Radford for the Parktown Heritage, Johannesburg

[104] HC 19.4.1941

[105] AA 5th series, vol.xix, 1991, 109-17

[106] His heir, also Charles Potts, came from Ollerton, nr Knutsford, Cheshire, and kept some of the property in Corbridge

[107] This was originally the Derwentwater pew, which was enlarged in 1725. The 1st Earl, though Catholic, was churchwarden, 1684-90. (NRO EP 57/25). In the days before Catholic Emancipation (1829) it was prudent, and less expensive in fines, to conform.

[108] NRO EP 57/49. Miscellaneous notes on Corbridge church

[109] Forster, op.cit., 88 fn.

[110] Forster, op.cit.,98ff; Ellerington, op.cit.,26; The Parish Magazine March 1909 (extracts from a letter to Canon Henry Lonsdale by C.G.Grey);

and The Bridge, May 1967

[111] HC 2.10.1867

[112] DDR/EJ/FAC/1/1282. Ralph Hedley, the celebrated Newcastle artist and carver, died in June 1913. Under the terms of his Will, the business was continued (until 1965) by two of his sons, Roger and Fred, and was known as 'Ralph Hedley Artistic and Architectural Carver'. Roger specialized in figure carving and masonry, Fred in decorative wood carving. John Millard, *Ralph Hedley, Tyneside Painter*, 1990

[113] NRO Queen Anne's Bounty, series 1, no 5: Corbridge 1831

[114] NRO Queen Anne's Bounty, series 2, no 12: Corbridge, 25.1.1887

[115] Craster, op.cit.,168,199

[116] HC 29.1.1881

[117] HC 4.9.1867.

[118] J.S.Maclean, *Newcastle and Carlisle Railway,* 1948, and articles in the *Railway Magazine* dated January 1934 and May 1936; also Silver Jubilee Supplement to HC 9.3.1935

[119] G.Whittle, *Newcastle and Carlisle Railway,* 1979, quoting Gordon Biddle, *Victorian Stations*, 1973

[120] HC 14.8.1867

[121] Information from Dr W. Cunningham

[122] Voluntary Aid Detachment nurses. These were volunteer nurses, without formal qualifications

[123] W.S.Gibson, op.cit.,105-6

[124] W.Henderson: *Folklore of Northern Counties of England and the Borders*, 1866, 84

[125] Markham, *Husbandry of Beasts* (1623), quoted in Bonser, op.cit.,101

[126] Forster, op.cit., 45

[127] Raine, Test.Ebor., quoted in Craster, op.cit.,201

[128] Letter from J.R.Harris, Professor of Egyptology, Univ. of Copenhagen, to Mr Michael White, 5.9.1971, in which he says he thinks it 'highly probable' that a sculpture built into the Viney museum wall is a fragment of a mourning Attis identified by Bruton, *Roman Fort at Manchester*, 1909, as coming from the 'Vicarage Stable'. The 'stable' was not, however, that belonging to the present Vicarage but to the building that preceded it which was destroyed in 1831. See p.101

[129] John Clayton had died in 1890 and his heir was his nephew, Nathaniel George. His widow, Mrs N.G.Clayton, died in 1927 and inherited the estate and Roman remains from her husband for her lifetime. She was connected by marriage to, and a great friend of, Alice Straker of Stagshaw House. It seems probable that she gave the objects from Chesters to Alice Straker for the Viney Museum (now mostly returned). Information from granddaughter of Mrs Clayton, Mrs R.Browne-Swinburne.

[130] HC 9.11.1929.

[131] HC 18.2.1928

[132] Most of this information is from the relevant issues of the *Hexham Courant*. Reporters, but not the public, were admitted. The minutes, held in NRO EP57/29, are usually very brief

[133] Ellerington, op.cit.,31

[134] HC 28.3.1914

[135] HC 17.8.1895

[136] HC 29. 5.1897

[137] HC 16.2.1901

[138] HC 9.11.1901

H.H.E.Craster, *History of Northumberland*, vol.x, Corbridge

Nikolaus Pevsner, *Northumberland* (The Buildings of England) 1992, edited by John Grundy, Grace McCombie, Peter Ryder and Humphrey Welfare

D.Archer, *Land of Singing Waters*, 1992

G.Biddle, *Victorian Stations*, 1973

C.J.Bates, *The Border Holds of Northumberland*, vol.i, 1891

M.C.Bishop, *Corstopitum: an Edwardian excavation*, 1994

John Blair, Richard Sharpe (eds) *Pastoral Care Before the Parish*, 1992; see also John Blair, *The Church in Anglo-Saxon Society* (forthcoming)

A.R.C. Bolton, *Six Brides of Dilston*, 1984

K.J. Bonser, *The Drovers, who they were and how they went*, 1970

J.E.Butler, *Memoir of John Grey of Dilston*, 1869

Tom Corfe (ed.) *Before Wilfrid, Britons, Romans and Anglo-Saxons in Tynedale*, 1997

S.F.Dixon, *History of the Saxon Royal Town of Corbridge-on-Tyne*, 1912

M.Ellerington, *A Brief History and Guide of Corbridge. c.1886*

English Heritage, *Corbridge Site Guide,* 1989

R.Forster, *A History of Corbridge and its Antiquities*, 1881

W.S.Gibson, *Historical Memoir of Northumberland...1862*

W.Henderson, *Folklore of the Northern Counties of England and the Borders*, 1866

J.S.Maclean, *Newcastle and Carlisle Railway*, 1948

Dennis Radford, 'Frank Emley', in series Architects of Parktown, Johannesburg, c.1989

Robert Robson, *Bob's Bridges, jottings from a Northumbrian foreman's diaries*, 1998

R.Selkirk, *On the Trail of the Legions*, 1995

R. Selkirk *Chester-le-Street and its Place in History,* 2001

D.P.Seymour, *Historical Buildings in South Africa* 1989

Jack Simmons (ed.) *Journeys in England, an anthology* 1951

W.W. Tomlinson, *Comprehensive Guide to Northumberland,* 10th edn 1923

G.Whittle, *Newcastle and Carlisle Railway*, 1979

Archaeologia Aeliana, Proceedings of the Society of Antiquaries of Newcastle upon Tyne, *Hexham Herald*, the *Hexham Courant* and *Newcastle Courant*